Wye Valley

40 Hill & Riverside Walks

AF083743

The author and publisher have made every effort to ensure that the information in this publication is accurate, and accept no responsibility whatsoever for any loss, injury or inconvenience experienced by any person or persons whilst using this book.

published by
pocket mountains ltd
The Old Church, Annanside, Moffat,
Dumfries and Galloway DG10 9HB
www.pocketmountains.com

ISBN: 978-1-916739-08-6

Text and photography copyright © Ben Giles. First published 2009, revised 2025

The right of Ben Giles to be identified as the Author of this work has been asserted by him in accordance with the Copyright, Designs and Patents Act 1988

A catalogue record for this book is available from the British Library

Contains Ordnance Survey data © Crown copyright and database right 2009

All rights reserved. No part of this publication may be reproduced, stored in a retrieval system, or transmitted in any form or by any means, electronic or mechanical, including photocopying and recording, unless expressly permitted by Pocket Mountains Ltd.

Printed by J Thomson Colour Printers, Glasgow

Introduction

Since 1971 the Wye Valley has been designated an Area of Outstanding Natural Beauty (AONB), covering on average an 8km-wide corridor from just south of Hereford in the north to Chepstow in the south. The lower Wye Valley, which has the AONB as its core, divides the lowlands of southern England and the uplands of South Wales, and incorporates significant parts of three counties, Herefordshire, Gloucestershire, and Monmouthshire. From the broad riverside meadows of the Herefordshire plain to the soaring limestone cliffs of the lower gorge near Chepstow, from the industrial heritage of the Forest of Dean in the east to the far-reaching views of the Trellech plateau in the west, the landscape of the lower Wye Valley can claim to be one of the most varied and picturesque places in Britain to explore on foot.

The Wye Valley has long claimed to be the birthplace of British tourism. At the end of the 18th century, tourists in search of the picturesque came to experience the dramatic river scenery on a two-day boat trip from Ross to Chepstow, in what became known as the Wye Tour. At the same time, it was also an industrial centre producing iron ore, coal, wire, paper, bark for tanning, and timber for the building of ships and cathedrals. In this connection the Forest of Dean has looked both east to the Severn and west to the Wye. The flotilla of boat tours and the spoils of the industrial age may have long since faded, but their effects and influence have not been completely effaced. One of the joys of walking in an area with such a rich past is stumbling across the reminders of past inhabitants and the lives they led.

About this guide

This guide contains 40 circular routes, covering an area somewhat broader than the AONB but within similar north-south boundaries. This collection of walks is split into five areas: Hereford Lowlands and the Woolhope Dome; Archenfield and the Monnow and Trothy Valleys; the Wye Gorge; the Forest of Dean; the Trellech to Chepstow Plateau. In part, the areas reflect the diverse geology and ecology of the landscape, but they are in no way essentially distinct or separate. Each has its own particular attractions and character, but there is much that is shared between all five areas.

Most of the routes are intended as comfortable walks or strolls, manageable by all willing to put one foot in front of another, at most requiring half a day to complete. Occasionally, the cumulative ascent may leave unseasoned legs a little stiffer, but in general the walking is on well-worn paths, lanes and tracks, which should require minimal time and effort for route-finding. However, the sketch maps serve an illustrative purpose and it is recommended that the relevant OS 1:25,000 map is carried – just two are needed to cover all areas (OS Explorers

OL14 and 189), both of which are readily available in local shops. For those who enjoy full day walks, some routes can readily be lengthened, while others can be combined for a longer excursion. The recommended time given for each walk is an estimate based on average walking speed, with an allowance added in for ascent and the type of ground. This will vary significantly, with individual ability and preference as well as the seasonal effects on conditions underfoot – especially across fields. It is hoped that there is plenty of interest along the routes themselves and it would be very possible to spread a short walk over a half day; conversely, most routes are short enough to attempt two in a day.

Getting around and accommodation

The main towns of the lower Wye Valley are Hereford, Ross-on-Wye, Monmouth and Chepstow. All are on regular bus routes, while train stations are located at Hereford and Chepstow. An effort has been made to include walks which can be reached by using local bus services. However, many of the outlying rural areas are only intermittently served on both a weekly and seasonal basis. Further information is available from traveline.info. Parking in small villages and hamlets can be a sensitive issue, but there are often areas designated for visitors. Pubs and inns are usually very accommodating, especially if the intention is to visit before or after a walk. Cycling is becoming increasingly popular in the area, and it would be feasible to combine the two activities, especially in the Forest of Dean which has an extensive network of cycle tracks. For accommodation, the area is well served by hotels, guesthouses and B&Bs, both in towns and villages and also in the surrounding countryside. In addition, there are campsites, youth hostels and even wigwams available.

Access and dogs

The Wye Valley is an area of mixed farming, with arable, dairy and sheep farming all present. At lambing time, farmers request that dogs are kept on leads. The presence of dogs for cows with calves can be problematic and it is not unheard of for cattle to behave in a very protective way. Even without a dog, cows which have recently calved should be left well alone. If in doubt, it is usually advisable and possible to find a short detour to avoid livestock. Most paths covered in the routes are well used and well maintained by various agencies, but in spring and summer hedges and undergrowth grow vigorously and nettles and brambles can infiltrate narrower paths and stile crossings.

A perspective on the landscape

To a Neolithic farmer, pausing at the end of a day on the steep slopes above the gorge of the, as yet unnamed, River Wye some 5000 years ago, the view westwards would have been filled with the sight of a rolling plateau of wooded hills, marked here and there by the rising smoke from wood fires, and framed on the horizon by the silhouetted shadows of black mountains. He might well have shuddered at venturing into the valley below and braving its waters wandering beneath towering cliffs. More likely he would have preferred to head southeast over a more thickly-wooded plateau on well-worn trackways to the salty waters of the large estuary to trade his surplus food for pottery, flints and luxuries.

On returning, should he suddenly have found himself in the 21st century, what might have caught his immediate attention is the probable increase in tree cover on the slopes of the valley below. True, above there would be more clearings and fields; perhaps he would nod in agreement with Wordsworth's appreciation of 'lines of Sportive wood run wild'. The rumblings from the valley of commuter and daytripper traffic and the chainsaws of the Forestry Commission would have been unidentifiable to him, but so too would they have been to the Wye tourists of the 18th century – the road was only constructed in 1824, in places still requiring continual efforts to keep it from sliding into the river, and many woods were then still managed by coppicing. The towers and spires of churches and the unnatural lines of quarrying would perhaps have arrested his eye and the transformation of trackways into tarmac would have felt strange underfoot. But he would have been as puzzled and inquisitive as any modern walker on discovering mile after mile of moss-covered drystone walls or the crumbled remains of a charcoal-burner's or miner's cottage now invaded by roots and creepers, let alone the rusting remains of iron bridges extending to tunnelled openings in the hillside or the arresting sight of so many dwellings, and what dwellings, gathered together on the floodplains of the river. And what to make of the thundering tide on the A40's dual carriageways?

And yet he might, just, despite the millennia of difference and change, have managed an amazed but quizzical smile on seeing that the line of the landscape was still, in essence, recognisable.

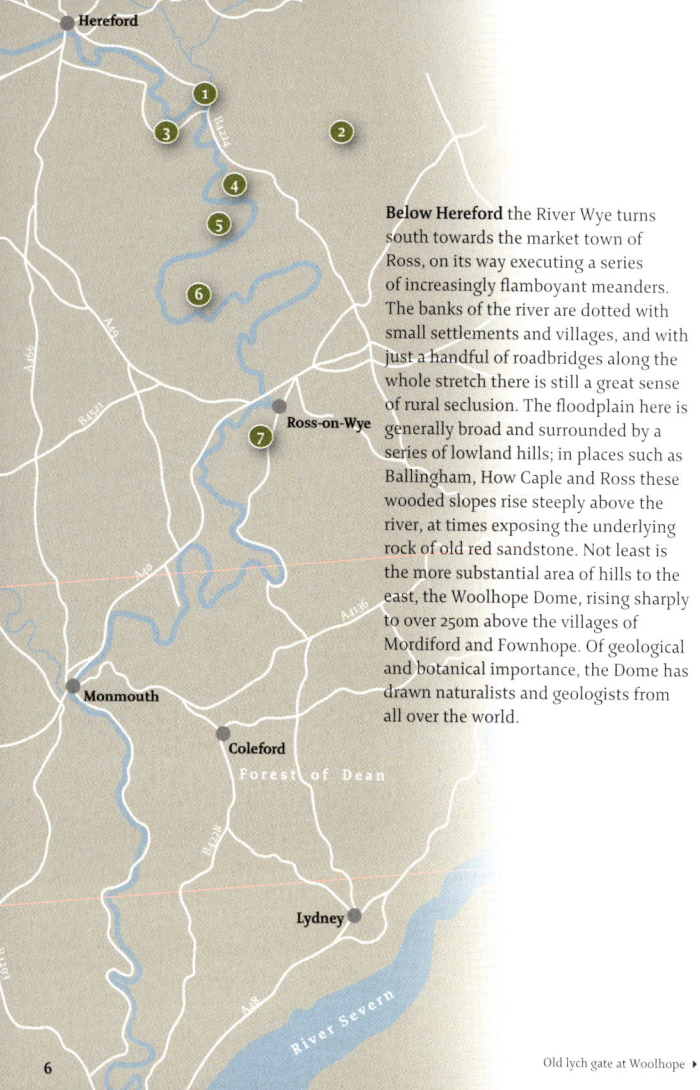

Below Hereford the River Wye turns south towards the market town of Ross, on its way executing a series of increasingly flamboyant meanders. The banks of the river are dotted with small settlements and villages, and with just a handful of roadbridges along the whole stretch there is still a great sense of rural seclusion. The floodplain here is generally broad and surrounded by a series of lowland hills; in places such as Ballingham, How Caple and Ross these wooded slopes rise steeply above the river, at times exposing the underlying rock of old red sandstone. Not least is the more substantial area of hills to the east, the Woolhope Dome, rising sharply to over 250m above the villages of Mordiford and Fownhope. Of geological and botanical importance, the Dome has drawn naturalists and geologists from all over the world.

Old lych gate at Woolhope ▶

Herefordshire Lowlands and the Woolhope Dome

1 **The Mordiford loop** 8
Watch out for dragons and bears hiding in these wooded hills

2 **Woolhope and Marcle Hill** 10
Gain your bearings with views in every direction on this undulating route

3 **Holme Lacy riverside wander** 12
Explore tranquil riverside meadows, once filled with busy rural and estate life

4 **Fownhope and Capler Camp** 14
A perfect mix of river and hill gives a more strenuous outing

5 **Ballingham village circular** 16
An enjoyable stroll through an ancient village perched above the river

6 **King's Caple and Foy meanders** 18
Time to stride out beside and then above this winding stretch of the Wye

7 **Ross-on-Wye and Chase Wood** 20
A more challenging route from an historic riverside town

The Mordiford loop

Distance 7km **Time** 2-3 hours
Terrain fields and woodland paths
Map OS Explorer 189 **Access** buses to Mordiford from Hereford

From the riverside village of Mordiford climb up into the rolling limestone country of the Woolhope Dome, an area famous for its varied natural history, before meandering back along the pretty Pentaloe Brook.

The bridge at Mordiford dates back to the 14th century and is one of the oldest bridges in Herefordshire. Before then the crossing of the River Lugg was by way of an ancient ford. A little above the bridge is the confluence of the River Frome, and a few hundred metres below the Lugg joins the Wye. From the bridge the impressive red-brick rectory can be seen and nearby is the church, dedicated to the Holy Rood, which dates in origin from Norman times and contains a Record of Occurrence of 27th May 1811, recording the details of a catastrophic flood of the Pentaloe Brook, which flows into the Lugg just below the bridge.

At the far end of the village, near the Moon Inn, a minor road leads east towards Haugh Wood and Woolhope. After 200m take the signed footpath on the left uphill through woodland, out into fields and on to the top of the hill. From here a grassy track takes you northwards on top of a broad ridge with wonderful views of Backbury Hill.

In the woodland ahead, a right turn leads to a lane and a little way along it a bridleway strikes up Backbury Hill, once the site of an Iron Age hillfort though now covered in woodland and gorse. The path soon levels out and contours round the south side of the hill before descending to Broomy Green and a junction with a forestry track into a conifer plantation.

Here, dog-leg right and then left at the

◂ Ruined timber-framed cottage above Pentaloe Brook

first house down over fields with stunning views ahead. At the lane a left turn leads to the hamlet of Checkley and the Pentaloe Brook. A path now heads southwest over a series of fields, with the brook never far away on the left, and then enters Bears Wood, so called as it is reputedly where the last brown bear was killed in Herefordshire. The route is often muddy here and soon crosses the stream at a bridge, but it may not be worth washing the mud off your boots yet.

Continue by the brook and at a clearing bear right. The brook soon bends away from the path; after 150m look out for the signed path which leads right out of the woodland into a field, down past a derelict timber-framed house to a field-edge track and the brook.

There is a legend that a Wyevern, a green dragon, used to descend from the woods above the village to devour livestock and people. In one version the dragon was befriended by a little girl, but the alarmed villagers persuaded a condemned criminal to try to kill the dragon in return for a pardon. Hiding in a cider barrel where the dragon came down to the river to drink, he shot it with an arrow, but the dragon had its revenge while still alive by incinerating the condemned man with its last breath.

Bear left with the brook and soon the houses of Pentaloe Close appear ahead. Aim diagonally right across the field to the edge of the housing and follow the waymarks through the estate to the road. Here, turn right to return to Mordiford.

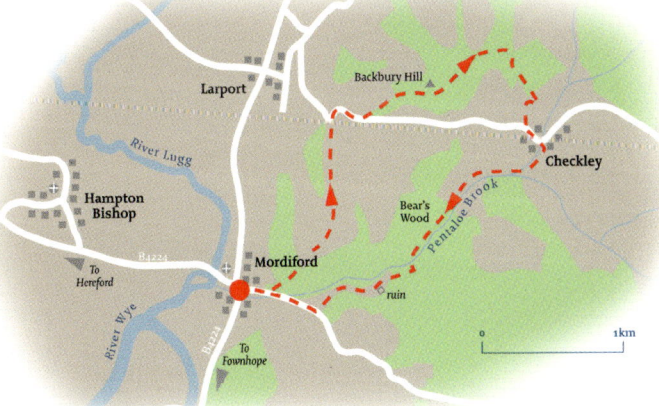

Woolhope and Marcle Hill

Distance 10km **Time** 3 hours
Terrain undulating fields and lanes
Map OS Explorer 189 **Access** buses to Woolhope from Hereford

Explore the rolling countryside at the heart of the Woolhope Dome and experience views at their best from the ridge along Marcle Hill.

Woolhope is located to the southeast of Hereford in the middle of steep-sided hills known as the Woolhope Dome, an area with a unique geological background. It also gave its name to The Woolhope Club. Founded in 1851 as the Woolhope Naturalists' Field Club, its interests now cover the local history, archaeology, and architecture of Herefordshire, as well as natural history and geology; its headquarters and Club Library are in the Woolhope Room in Hereford Library.

The walk starts from the centre of Woolhope by the lych gate to the church and the Crown Inn.

Walk eastwards out of the village, towards Putley, down the hill with views of Marcle Hill ahead, passing Court Farm, and take the first lane on the right just before the Butchers Arms pub, a black and white timbered house. Where the lane bends left, keep on uphill through Beans Butts Wood, past buildings to a field above. From the top of the field there are extensive views back to the Black Mountains and into Mid Wales. Here, the underlying rock of Silurian limestone, some 400 million years old, contrasts with the old red sandstone found in much of the nearby Wye river valley and gives rise to the paler soils underfoot as well as the variety of woodland, wildflower meadows and extensive hedgerows.

Cross into Busland Wood, an ancient woodland full of bluebells in spring, and descend to a field and across a dry valley up to the road at Hooper's Oak. Turn right along the ridge, which has been in use as a travellers' route since the Bronze Age.

◀ Cascades near Whittlebury Farm

There are extensive views northeastwards to the Malvern Hills and southeastwards to the Cotswolds. Where the road bends left at a junction, take the path ahead up steps (just down from the junction is a picnic area and car park with a useful display board about the local geology). Continue along the ridge on a field-edge path for 2km, passing the high point of the ridge and then descending past a mast.

On reaching a delightful sunken trackway, turn right along the edge of Lyndalls Wood, downhill to where the track becomes a lane and soon after crosses a stream. Just round the left bend, take a path off right across fields to Whittlebury Farm, with its pretty stream and orchards. Cross the road and over two more fields with the stream nearby on the left, passing another Court Farm, a 15th-century manor house with interesting ornamental chimney stacks, to the tranquil church of Sollers Hope beyond. The current church dates from the 14th century, itself the restoration of a Saxon building, and was financed by the brother of Dick Whittington, the famous Mayor of London.

Leave the churchyard by the west gate and turn right across horse paddocks past the tump, a mound which is the remains of a Romano-British camp. Bear left with the stream and then up across fields to a gap between the alder-lined stream on the left and Long Wood on the right. Cross the stream and go over the brow of the hill to a stile, with views ahead to Woolhope. Here, turn left and soon cross a footbridge before bearing right into the adjacent field. Now make for the house ahead and onto a lane which passes Alford's Mill, a former cider mill. Wander along this pleasant lane, bearing left at a T-junction, for just over 1km back to Woolhope.

Holme Lacy riverside wander

Distance 8km **Time** 2 hours
Terrain riverside paths and parkland
Map OS Explorer 189 **Access** buses to Holme Lacy from Hereford

Stroll along the sweeping meanders of the River Wye to a lost medieval village, and through the grounds of one of the largest and oldest country houses in Herefordshire.

At the western edge of the village, the B4399 passes over the old Ross to Hereford railway line. From the bridge, where there is room for a few cars, you can look down into the deep cutting – enthusiasts can descend a short path and explore it – but the walk follows the signed field-path above the railway cutting northwards towards the River Wye and round the top of the field to the right. Depending on the season the river can be glimpsed through the trees at the bottom of the steep slope. The lower path at the river's edge has long been overgrown and eroded, an indication of the powerful meandering nature of the Wye below Hereford. Cross three more fields before descending through a small copse to the riverside.

The route now follows the river round its long meander. At the bend's apex the River Lugg slips with barely a murmur into the waters of the Wye and here the riverside meadows now stand empty, except for grazing livestock. Once, however, they would have been populated by people known as 'brinkers', property owners who fiercely defended their rights to fish the 'free waters' of the Wye. Further on is Holme Lacy Bridge, whose forerunner used to be adorned by some substantial spiked iron railings – an incentive to stop and pay the toll to cross the river; and for vehicles it is still one of only three crossing points over the Wye between Hereford and Ross.

Cross the road and continue by the river for 1.5km in the same direction round the next left bend to a lane, called Church Road. Here you can see low mounds and earthworks which may indicate the remains of a sizeable medieval village,

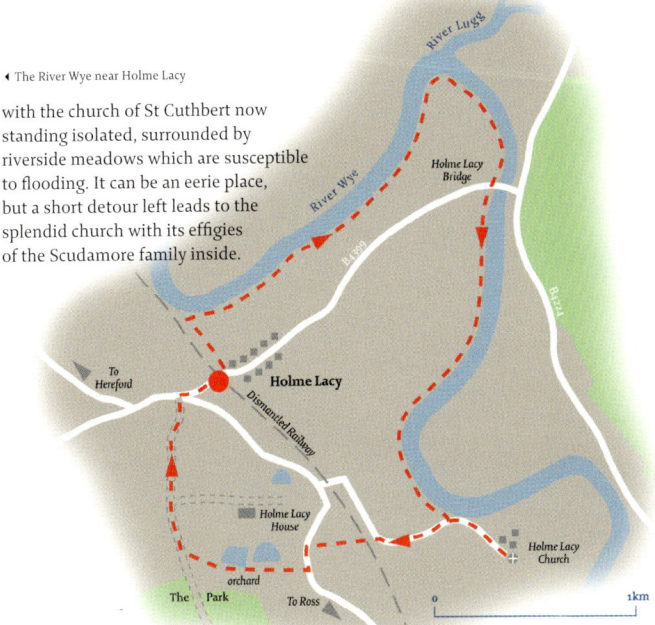

◀ The River Wye near Holme Lacy

with the church of St Cuthbert now standing isolated, surrounded by riverside meadows which are susceptible to flooding. It can be an eerie place, but a short detour left leads to the splendid church with its effigies of the Scudamore family inside.

Westwards along Church Road at the bend, the route passes through some cow-gates over the line of the disused railway and in the middle of the far side of the field crosses onto a road. A dog-leg left past the Old Schoolhouse and then right takes you into a pretty orchard.

At its top right corner is the parkland of Holme Lacy House, now a hotel but for much of the last century it was used as a psychiatric hospital. Before then it had been one of the seats of the Scudamore family, who now reside at Kentchurch Court near Grosmont. In fact, in the late 17th century the Scudamores had themselves pulled down an existing brick house, built in the reign of Henry III by the Lacy family who had originally come over to England with William the Conqueror. As you now pass the lake there is a sweeping view up to the house. At the top of the field, turn right onto a lane, past the delightful walled gardens and lodges of the house and parkland, back to the B4399 and Holme Lacy. Turn right here to reach the railway bridge.

Fownhope and Capler Camp

Distance 8km **Time** 2-3 hours
Terrain riverside and field paths, woodland, steep slopes around Capler Camp **Map** OS Explorer 189 **Access** buses to Fownhope from Hereford

A leisurely approach along the river, then a climb up to the lofty ramparts of Capler Camp, gives some of the most varied walking in this part of the Wye Valley.

Fownhope is an attractive village on the east bank of the River Wye and is worth exploring in its own right, not least if you happen to be visiting on Oak Apple Day at the start of June when a parade to celebrate Charles II's triumphant entry into London in 1660 finishes at the black and white timbered Green Man Inn, which has been a coaching inn and courthouse since the 15th century.

Ferry Lane leads down to the River Wye and serves as a reminder that the village was once an important port between Hereford and Ross. Barges used to carry bark for use in the tanning industry downstream to Lydbrook, where they would be reloaded with a return cargo of coal. Beyond Ferry Boat Cottage, bear left into fields and head south to reach the left bank of the Wye and on to Leabrink House, sited in a picturesque position on a bend in the river where fishing is popular.

The route now heads up over the shoulder of the hill, with views opening out to the south and west, to reach a stone barn before descending right to the floodplain once more. Bear left over fields to reach Mancell's Ferry, with views across the river to Ballingham Hill. Here was a popular crossing point, supervised at one time by a Mr Mancell who gave his name to the cottage. When the water is low enough, the former landing stages are clearly visible under the opposite bank and it is still a good place for a picnic.

The riverside path continues beyond the cottage and ahead is Capler Camp hillfort hidden in the trees. After 1km,

◂ Old water pump at Fownhope

reach Capler Wood and turn left uphill to the road, then right up to the viewpoint, with the trees providing welcome shade on a hot summer's day. Now the route turns northwards to pick up the Wye Valley Walk uphill and round the south side of Capler Camp, passing between the prominent earth ramparts to reach the stone buildings on its eastern edge. This is another Iron Age hillfort, one of many in the area, and it is superbly positioned to survey the low ground to the north, though there is now extensive tree cover. Ignore the track off right to the triangulation point and follow the Wye Valley Walk steeply down the north side of the hill to Caplor Farm.

Here, the route leaves the Wye Valley Walk and heads in a northwesterly direction over fields, along a right of way which starts at the back of the buildings at the lower end of the farm. Aim for the left of a pair of gates and a man-made lake before following the small stream for 200m. The route dog-legs left, then right before heading over the rise and down to a footbridge over a stream and up to the walled garden of derelict Nash Farm. In the far left corner of this field, cross a stile and in 50m go right over another stile down to a gate by a telegraph pole and the house beyond. Here, the right of way bears right along the driveway to the road where a right turn leads to Fownhope past the church, with the remains of its combined stocks and whipping post in the churchyard wall.

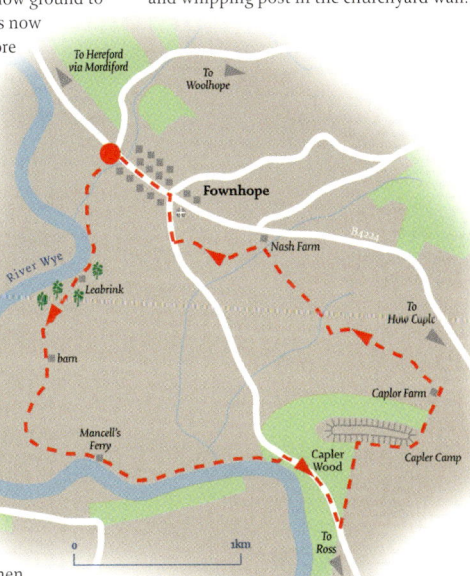

Ballingham village circular

Distance 4km **Time** 1 hour 30
Terrain riverside path, woodland and lanes, with a steep descent to the river
Map OS Explorer 189 **Access** no public transport to the start

Step back in time and enjoy this now tranquil countryside, which once thronged with busy rural life.

Ballingham is now a quiet village tucked away to the west of one of the sweeping loops of the River Wye between Hereford and Ross. As with many villages in this part of Herefordshire its population has diminished over the last hundred years, though there are hints of its former significance, such as Ballingham Hall whose stone frontage and gables can be seen from the end of the lane by the church. The blank panels with their ovals are a sign of its origin from the years after the Restoration in 1660, and the adjacent modern farm buildings highlight the agricultural changes that have taken place in more recent years.

The walk itself starts from the sandstone church of St Dubricius, a Celtic saint of the 6th century, and goes up the lane past the village hall, formerly the school, towards the centre of the village, with its green and pond. The lane opposite leads to Ballingham Chapel, a 20th-century construction, and beyond to the ancient settlement of Ballingham Hill. The left fork is known as Saycells Path and it leads to the farm of the same name. The Saycells are a family whose earliest recorded connection with the village stretches back to the 13th century and the whole place still has the feel of working countryside, though the throngs of agricultural workers have long gone.

Near the top of the lane, before the farm at a path T-junction, turn right down

◂ St Dubricius' churchyard at Ballingham

past a house and then descend steeply along the edge of woodland and across the lane known as the King's Way, a medieval route which still runs parallel to the River Wye. Here, turn downstream along the riverbank, passing Mancell's Ferry house opposite. This is a good place to stop for a riverside picnic. The path soon enters Ballingham Wood where it meets the river.

At the far end of the wood, keep to the right-hand side of the field, still following the edge of Ballingham Wood, with good views ahead to Capler Hill and its hillfort. At the wood's eastern end, bear right through a gate and climb steps steadily back uphill along the southern edge of the wood in a westerly direction, from where the spire of Ballingham church can be seen across the fields.

The brambles lining the edge of the wood here are good for blackberrying in late summer or early autumn. The path passes through a gate and along the edge of a field to reach the road. Here a left turn uphill brings you to the buildings of Dunn's Farm and Mayview Farm, from where a path through the hedge on the left leads over the field in the direction of the church – there are often cows here with calves; if so, it might be an idea to follow the lane to the village centre and retrace your steps past the village hall to the church.

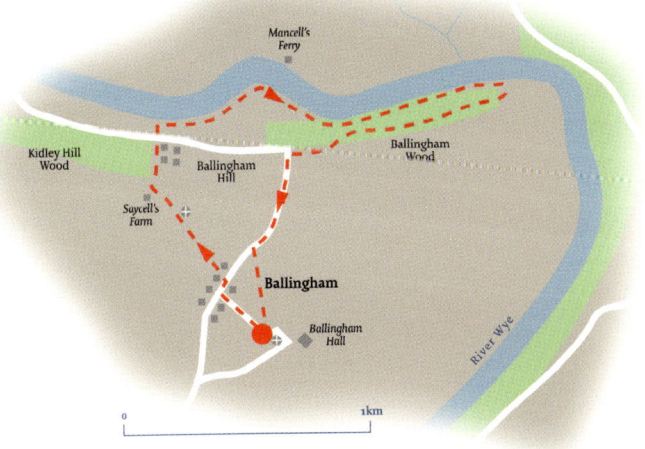

King's Caple and Foy meanders

Distance 15km **Time** 4-5 hours **Terrain** field paths and lanes **Map** OS Explorer 189 **Access** buses to King's Caple (request stop) from Hereford and Ross

This walk weaves its way among some of the largest meanders of the River Wye, crossing the river on picturesque footbridges and passing through several pretty hamlets.

The church in King's Caple occupies the former bailey of a Norman castle whose motte, known as Caple Tump, stands opposite. Some years ago in the churchyard near the cross a grim discovery was made of a plague pit, probably dating to the Black Death of 1348. The walk heads towards the centre of the village along what was once a Roman Road known as Caple Street, passing the impressive red-brick King's Caple Court. The name of the house and village recall that local allegiance was once directly to the kings of England, rather than to the ecclesiastical authority of nearby Hereford Cathedral.

At the crossroads turn right (signposted for Sellack Boat) down the lane and at the sharp left bend continue ahead to the River Wye and across the suspension bridge, which was paid for by public subscription in 1895 and replaced the old ferry and ford – a story is still told about the vicar who, in order to carry out his ministry with dry feet, used to criss-cross the river on stilts. Across the fields is Sellack, with its prominent church and a rare dedication to St Tysilio. From here, the route turns left uphill along quiet lanes through Baysham to Strangford Farm. Beyond, a tractor track leads over fields along the top of the broad ridge for just over 1km, with panoramic views

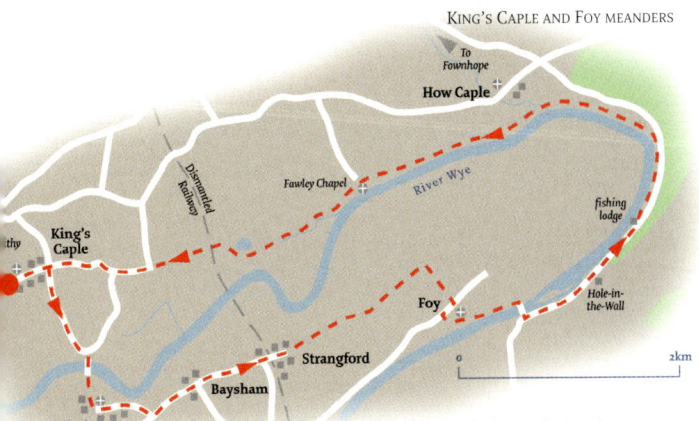

over the river valley and the surrounding hills. Where the track bends left downhill, continue ahead for 150m, then right through a gate and down to the lane at Foy, before turning right for the church.

St Mary's is built in a commanding position overlooking the river and its setting is made grander by the proximity of the 18th-century vicarage, Foye Hall. Inside the church are memorials to the Abrahall family, along with some curious images of hedgehogs. The walk now crosses the field at the rear of the church to the river, a pleasant place to pause for a rest or picnic, and follows it upstream to cross Foy Bridge, another elegant suspension bridge, this one built in 1921 after the previous bridge was washed away by a flood. A left turn along the route of the Wye Valley Walk soon reaches the small hamlet of Hole-in-the-Wall, whose unusual name probably recalls the siting of a post-house here in the 19th century, though some talk of a tunnel below the Wye linking religious houses as the origin of the name. A little beyond, just before a cattle grid, the way bears left down to the riverside again, with a balconied fishing lodge on the opposite bank, and on to How Caple.

The onward route leaves the Wye Valley Walk just beyond the bridge and turns left through a field-gate uphill, passing to the right of the house ahead and continuing in a WSW direction up over fields and down to Seabournes Farm at Fawley. A detour downhill leads to the private Fawley Chapel and Fawley Court, once the home of John Kyrle, the famous benefactor of Ross. Across the lane and past the cowsheds, a bridleway leads into the fields beyond. After 1km, in the third field, the path descends left and then bears round to the right over the outflow of a small lake, before passing through a tunnel under the disused Ross to Hereford railway and up one more field to a cottage. Here, a left turn onto the lane soon leads back to the houses of King's Caple.

◂ Suspension bridge at Foy

Ross-on-Wye and Chase Wood

Distance 10km **Time** 3-4 hours
Terrain riverside paths, fields and steep slopes in Chase Wood
Map OS Explorer 189 **Access** buses to Ross-on-Wye from Monmouth and Hereford

Retrace the river courses, ancient and modern, around Ross before an ascent to the top of Chase Wood.

As 'Gate of the Wye', Ross has long been associated with the river that winds its way across the low ground to the west. Indeed, an ancient river meander south of Chase Wood suggests that millions of years ago the sandstone outcrop on which the town stands would have been almost surrounded by the river. Nowadays there are still extensive floods, though the town has also long been known for its reliable climate and houses one of the oldest weather stations in the country. The centre of Ross is dominated by the red sandstone of the Market House, from where the walk starts.

At the far end of the High Street, use Wye Street to descend to the river. The riverside path leads downstream to Wilton, with its bridge and castle across the water. The castle was a casualty of the Royalists in the Civil War; its siting on low ground is curious, but it predates the late 16th-century bridge by at least 300 years, so it most likely guarded an ancient ford here. The path continues over the bridge, with an old river cliff away to the left, and after 1km veers away from the river to the corner of the wood ahead. You soon cross the driveway of Cubberley House, beyond which a field-edge path leads to The Homme farm.

Turn left down the farm's driveway and right at the road, soon passing a cross in woodland on the right and Hom Green Chapel on the left – the 'Cross in the Woodland' is of unknown origin but may mark the site of an old chapel. Just past the entrance to Hill Court, the route turns left

Ross-on-Wye and Chase Wood

up the driveway to the picturesque black and white timbers of Old Hill Court and a lane beyond. A dog-leg right then left takes you over the fields of Coughton Marsh, with views to Chase Wood ahead on the left and Howle Hill on the right. The gap marks the line of the ancient meander of the River Wye. Now supporting fruit-growing, the whole of this low-lying area used to be the river's watercourse. On passing under electricity lines bear slightly right and the path soon reaches the B4234. Here, a detour right for 500m leads to the entrance to Coughton Marsh SSSI, a small area of marsh woodland of historical and biological interest because it is the only area of plateau alder woodland left in the lower Wye Valley.

The walk bears left into Coughton, right at the bend (signposted for Howle Hill) and through the village, which now occupies the ancient riverbed, passing a former cider house which used also to be the tollhouse when this turnpike road was first built. Just before the last buildings, turn left onto the route of the Wye Valley Walk. Head up across fields into Chase Wood, where the path ascends very steeply to the hillfort at the top, and round its east side on which the earthworks are well-defined. Towards the north end, the track descends, with views to the Malvern Hills, past Hill Farm into Merivale Wood, a wildlife reserve managed by Herefordshire Nature Trust. Just beyond the entrance-gate turn left, off the Wye Valley Walk, onto a path which winds its way down through the wood, steeply at times, to a track at the bottom. Turn right to a metal kissing-gate and then left along the field edge, with views left to Garway Hill.

Cross over the line of the disused railway and continue into the housing estate, bearing right along Merivale Lane past Merivale House. At the T-junction turn left and then right at the top of this road to return to the centre of Ross.

◂ Looking across river meadows to Ross-on-Wye

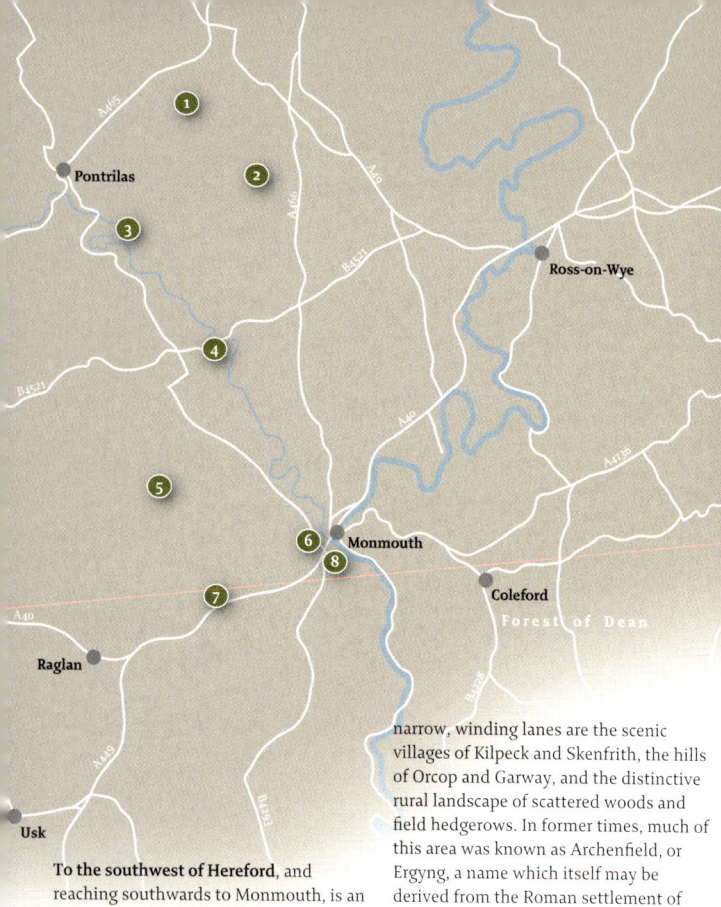

To the southwest of Hereford, and reaching southwards to Monmouth, is an ancient area of rolling hills and river valleys. Bounded on the north by the Worm Brook and in the east by the Wye river valley, it encloses an area extending southwards to the Monnow and Trothy Valleys. Hidden amongst its maze of narrow, winding lanes are the scenic villages of Kilpeck and Skenfrith, the hills of Orcop and Garway, and the distinctive rural landscape of scattered woods and field hedgerows. In former times, much of this area was known as Archenfield, or Ergyng, a name which itself may be derived from the Roman settlement of Ariconium at Weston under Penyard near Ross. It was a Welsh enclave, largely within what is now Herefordshire, where Welsh was spoken up to the start of the 20th century, testament to which is the number of places still with Welsh names.

Old road sign at Dingestow ▶

Archenfield and the Monnow and Trothy Valleys

1 **Inn and out of Kilpeck** 24
There is plenty to see in this rightly popular village before enjoying the surrounding fields and lanes

2 **The Garren Valley and Orcop Hill** 26
Solitude is guaranteed at the heart of Archenfield's hidden rolling countryside

3 **Garway Hill and Jack O'Kent** 28
One of the best hills west of the Wye, set in the secluded Monnow Valley

4 **Skenfrith and Llanrothal** 30
Walk in the steps of medieval bargemen from one of the prettiest villages in South Wales

5 **The Trothy and the lost abbey** 32
Riverside meadows and views of the hills are at their best here

6 **Monmouth and the King's Wood** 34
From the oldest fortified bridge in Britain, scale the wooded heights to the west of this historic town

7 **Dingestow and the Trothy** 36
The proximity of village, river, country house and woodland makes for a memorable outing

8 **The lost treasures of Troy** 38
Leave plenty of time to take in the views and seclusion at Penallt, high above the Wye Valley

Inn and out of Kilpeck

Distance 3km **Time** 1 hour **Terrain** lanes and fields **Map** OS Explorer 189 **Access** buses from Hereford and Abergavenny stop at Wormbridge on the A465, 2km west of Kilpeck

Stroll around one of Herefordshire's most historic villages before circling the ancient fields and woods to the south. This route is short enough to be ideal before, or after, a visit to the pub.

Kilpeck is one of the most celebrated and popular villages in Herefordshire. Its church draws visitors from far afield and there is plenty to look at. The semi-circular apse at the east end hints at its Norman origins, but the carvings on the doorway of its south porch and the corbel table beneath the eaves are what most come to see. There are 85 grotesque medieval motifs to spot and some gaps where a number of others have been removed over the centuries, perhaps from a more modern sense of propriety.

To the east of the church stands the remains of a Norman motte and bailey castle whose walls and moat invite exploration. To the north is a helpful information board and viewing spot, from where the outline of the ancient village stockade can be traced.

The village is a delight to wander through and, though the school has long since closed, the local pub, the Kilpeck Inn, welcomes walkers. Just by the old school, beyond the pub, a lane leads off

◀ The south door of St Mary's and St David's Church at Kilpeck

left and takes you up the hill. Many of the lanes in this area connect with the old trackway that runs along the ridge ahead. Its antiquity can only be guessed at, but it may well stretch back to the Bronze Age or even to Neolithic times.

The lane meanders uphill and in 350m there is a track off right which leads to Dippersmoor Farm. Just before the buildings take the path left, off the track and into the adjacent field, and pass above an old timber and brick long barn. The farm was originally Dippersmoor Manor and of interest architecturally as it is of 15th-century cruck construction, where both the walls and the roof are supported on huge curved beams.

Continue across the field to the rear of the buildings, through a gap into a second one and curve round to the right above a delightful tree-lined dell. This is a game and wildlife conservation area and it is requested that dogs are kept on a lead here. The path now reaches Dippersmoor Wood and bears right along its southern edge, with views ahead to the ridges of the Black Mountains – and with the sun setting behind these hills it is perhaps easy to see how they got their name. At the bottom of this field, bear left along the hedge for 50m and then turn right through a gate into the field below.

In the bottom right-hand corner of this field, the path leads northeastwards for 500m, alongside a hedge over a further three fields, to reach the road just to the south of Kilpeck. Here, turn right and soon reach the old school and the centre of the village.

The Garren Valley and Orcop Hill

Distance 4km **Time** 1 hour
Terrain undulating lanes and fields
Map OS Explorer 189 **Access** buses from Hereford to Orcop Hill

Wander among the hidden folds and meadows of the Garren Valley. This one is great for kids and grown-ups – the only decision is before or after a visit to the pub.

Orcop Hill is one of the highest points on a chain of hills between the valleys of the River Monnow, to the south, and the Worm Brook, to the north. It is sited in often bypassed countryside, equidistant from Hereford, Ross and Monmouth 18km away. This scattered settlement, which stretches south to Orcop village, used to have five pubs. Now, only the Fountain Inn remains. This pub traces its name to the nearby Copywell (or Coppice Well). Until the 1960s it was the main source of water in the area, requiring the inhabitants of the Garren Valley to ferry their water for a considerable distance.

The walk starts from the Baptist Chapel with its small graveyard opposite the inn and heads uphill, taking the first road on the left. Shortly, at a T-junction, bear left for 500m round the left bend and just beyond the driveway to Quarry Farm take a path left over a stile into a field. Follow the top edge of this field to a stile hidden in the far top corner. Cross into the next field, and bear left downhill and through the hedgeline into the field below. Here, the views open out to Orcop village and

round to Garway Hill as you descend southwest over more fields. Local folklore tells the story of how the inhabitants of this valley had a lucky escape from the devil. In one of their feuding contests, the giant Jack O'Kent and the devil were vying to dam the valley in order to make an enormous fishpond and they began ferrying huge boulders as they jumped from hilltop to hilltop. However, they dropped their stones while landing on the summit of Garway Hill. The stones rolled down the south side and the place where they came to rest has since been known as White Rocks.

As the slope levels off, go through a gateway to the far side of the field to reach a crosspaths. Here is the site of the former Stradway Farm – the buildings are still marked on the map, though the farmer dismantled the farmhouse some years ago and surprisingly little evidence remains of what was a substantial building and cider mill. On clear, sunny days it is a tranquil spot, ideal now for a picnic or rest. To continue, turn left across the stile towards the woodland ahead on the left, where the field narrows. The edge of the woodland leads to a stile at the bottom of the field into a copse. Cross over a stream and through the copse to a field. Here, turn left and follow the field edge with the stream on the left in trees.

The path soon crosses back over the stream, becoming a track which leads to and through Great Ynys Farm. Ynys is the Welsh word for 'island' and one theory for the origin of the name is that the stream from the Copywell once divided and flowed around both sides of the buildings, thus isolating the farm in mid-stream. The track now continues up to the road, where a left turn uphill soon reaches Orcop Hill.

◂ Looking south across the Garren Valley

ARCHENFIELD AND THE MONNOW AND TROTHY VALLEYS

Garway Hill and Jack O'Kent

Distance 9km **Time** 3-4 hours
Terrain lanes and fields; the high ground of Garway Hill can be confusing in mist
Map OS Explorer 189 **Access** no public transport to the start

Walk in the footsteps of the giant Jack O'Kent and see seven counties from the best viewpoint the Monnow Valley has to offer.

Jack O'Kent is a figure intimately associated with Kentchurch. Legend has it that he was a giant wizard in league with the devil who had sold his soul in exchange for supernatural powers and that he built the bridge over the Monnow below Grosmont in just a single night. He is said to have then tricked the devil out of the due payment of the first living soul to set foot on it by throwing a bone across, which was duly chased by a dog. Others tell the tale that he is buried in the very walls of the church, so that being 'neither in nor out' his soul might be confined and not snatched by the devil. In nearby Kentchurch Park, there is even his own oak tree, reputedly a thousand years old and the largest in the Wye Valley, with a girth of over 11m.

From the church 1km east of Grosmont Bridge, head north along the road and take the first right along a lane to Bannut Tree Farm, with Kentchurch Park on the right. Just beyond the farm, take the path off right, which rises to a line of mature oaks and alongside a former sunken trackway into a copse to pass below Court-a-Grove Farm. Now the route crosses a series of six fields uphill in an easterly and then ENE direction (in the second field bear slightly left into the dip and through a copse above some springs to cross a footbridge and stile into the next field).

On reaching the road, turn right and soon pass above a baptist chapel with views north to Aconbury Hill. When the

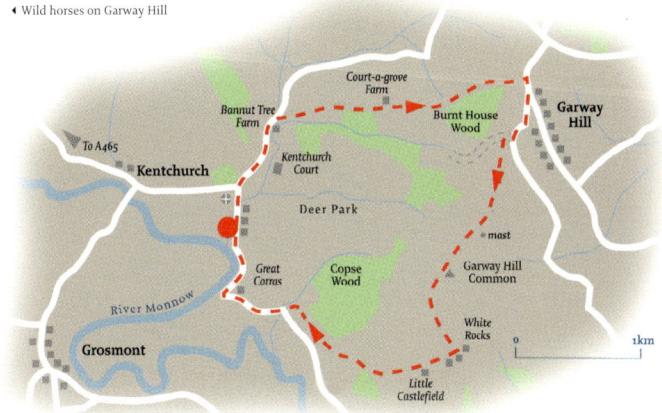

◀ Wild horses on Garway Hill

road bends back left and Garway Hill communications mast is seen ahead, turn right up a track. At the top of the rise, bear left up through woodland past the communications mast onto the open slopes of Garway Hill to its trig point and old pillbox. You can reputedly see seven counties on a clear day, but don't take your eye off your sandwiches as the white mountain horses and the sheep are wise to what visitors bring with them.

The horses survive on the common all year round, getting their water from nearby Black Pool, which not only mysteriously lasts all year with no visible spring but also provides a breeding ground for the rare and protected great-crested newt. The hill is a haven for wildlife and has never been ploughed. There are said to be over 70 species of bird, including skylark, song thrush and yellowhammer and it's a great habitat for butterflies.

Descend the far south side of the hill with views ahead to Dawn of the Day. On reaching the track near White Rocks – you might hear the 'hoo-hoo-hoo' or harsh 'kewick' of a thriving group of tawny owls here – turn right down past Little Castlefield, whose name recalls the former site of a Roman camp and road 1km to the southwest, near Castlefield Farm just above the Monnow. Now descend for just over 1km across fields, at first in a westerly direction, passing above Little Corras Farm with views ahead to the Black Mountains. Then bear more to the right and aim for the left edge of the woodland ahead, before dropping down to the left to reach the road. Here, turn right and follow the lane, known now to some as the 'English Road', for a little over 1km back to Kentchurch, passing an ancient ford over the River Monnow which is still used by farm vehicles.

Skenfrith and Llanrothal

Distance 9km **Time** 3 hours
Terrain riverside and woodland paths with a climb out of the Monnow Valley
Map OS Explorer OL14 **Access** no public transport to the start

Explore the historic village of Skenfrith before venturing down the secluded valley of the River Monnow.

Clustered round a bend of the River Monnow, the village of Skenfrith, with its castle and church, provides one of the most picturesque settings of Welsh rural life in existence today. Parking is available on what was once the stone-revetted moat of the medieval castle, one of the so-called trilateral castles (the others are Grosmont and White Castle), and there are a number of information boards to help with exploration.

Just beyond the pub, The Bell, the road to Ross crosses the River Monnow over the stone bridge, built in 1824 at a time when travel by coach and horse was still the only practical means of long-distance transport and a reminder of the pub's role as a coaching inn – the inaugural run of the world's first railway passenger service was still six years away. A path leads off right in a northeasterly direction over fields beside the river for 1.5km to the grounds of Sand House. Now it is a tranquil walk, thick with balsam in late summer, but the rediscovery of the medieval quay at Skenfrith Castle has pointed to the importance of the river as a means of transporting goods from Monmouth and beyond. It is likely that flat-bottomed barges would have been used, hauled upriver by horses or gangs of men in harness.

Passing in front of the house, bear left over a footbridge and left again into woodland to follow a waymarked path up the hill to the rear. As the path ascends beside a stream, look out for the small

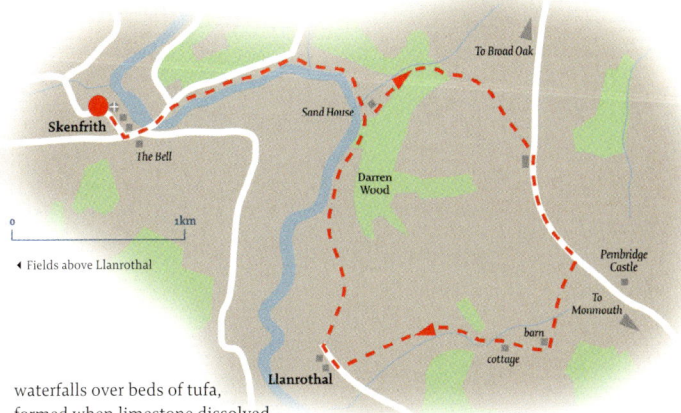

◀ Fields above Llanrothal

waterfalls over beds of tufa, formed when limestone dissolved in water is deposited on rocks and debris in the stream. Cross over a forestry track to continue uphill, through a gate and over a footbridge to a stile. Bear right and shortly leave the woodland to go over three fields in a southeasterly direction to the top of the hill with views back to Garway Hill and Dawn of the Day (go diagonally left up the first field or follow the right-hand edges if ploughed; in the third one aim for the bungalow).

At the road, turn right over the brow of the hill and down into the dip, with views northeast to the Malvern Hills and the Monnow Valley to the right. Ahead can be seen Pembridge Castle – a restored 13th-century fortified manor house and, in 1679, the scene of the arrest of the Catholic martyr John Kemble. By then an elderly priest, Kemble was implicated in Titus Oates' allegations of a papist plot to kill the king, Charles II. Arrested by John Scudamore of nearby Kentchurch, he was tried in London and then returned to Hereford to be hanged. One of Kemble's hands is still preserved at Hereford; his body rests nearby in the churchyard of St Mary's, Welsh Newton, and a pilgrimage to his grave is made every year.

From the dip, bear right through a field opening and take the lower of a pair of paths bearing right down to a stream in a wooded dell and into the field beyond. Pass under the electricity lines and in 50m go right through a field gate and continue to the barn ahead. A right turn beside the banked hedge leads down to a house and a track to Llanrothal.

At the lane, turn right and go past Llanrothal Court to a field gate. Now cross four fields, with the River Monnow nearby on the left, and continue into the woodland ahead, where a path soon brings you to Sand House once again. From here, the outward route is followed back to Skenfrith.

ARCHENFIELD AND THE MONNOW AND TROTHY VALLEYS

The Trothy and the lost abbey

Distance 4km **Time** 1 hour 30
Terrain lanes and fields, which can get muddy **Map** OS Explorer OL14
Access no public transport to the start

This short circuit takes in some of the most secluded and tranquil countryside the Trothy Valley has to offer, with pleasant walking by the river and great views from the ridge above.

Llanvihangel-Ystern-Llewern is one of the most out-of-the-way spots in the Trothy Valley and is found 8km west of Monmouth near Onen on the B4233 Abergavenny road. The name of the place most likely means 'St Michael's by the Marshy Bend of the River' and hints at its low-lying location near the River Trothy. There is room for a few cars to park just by the church. Offa's Dyke Path runs through here and the church is kept locked when not in use.

From the church, walk up the road to the bend and bear left on a track on the route of Offa's Dyke Path (ODP), with the River Trothy below on the left. After 300m, just before farm buildings, bear left across a footbridge into riverside meadows, which are liable to flooding and can be muddy in places in wet conditions. However, in dry conditions in spring and summer it makes for a picture-postcard stroll beside the twisting Trothy. After 750m, as the second field broadens out, look for a marker post by the river indicating a right turn up the steep bank to cut the corner of the third field.

The Trothy and the lost Abbey

◀ Above Llanvihangel-Ystern-Llewern looking west

Now, away from the river, continue on ODP over three more fields in a southeasterly direction to the road above Abbey Bridge. The name of the bridge recalls the siting, a little to the southeast, of former Grace Dieu Abbey. It was another Cistercian foundation but now, unlike nearby Tintern Abbey and Abbey Dore, not a stone of this retreat remains visible and its actual location is uncertain. Quite why Grace Dieu vanished is lost to history, but there still lingers the sense of isolation that the Cistercians must have been seeking in establishing a monastery in this valley.

Now turn right, off the route of ODP, uphill past Abbey Cottage and then right again, just over the brow of the hill, along a lane which rises and falls, giving good views of the surrounding countryside. After a little over 1km, at a junction, the lane bends uphill to the right (north) and passes through a delightful copse of woodland before descending, with views to the hills of the Skirrid and the Graig, round some steep bends to the start.

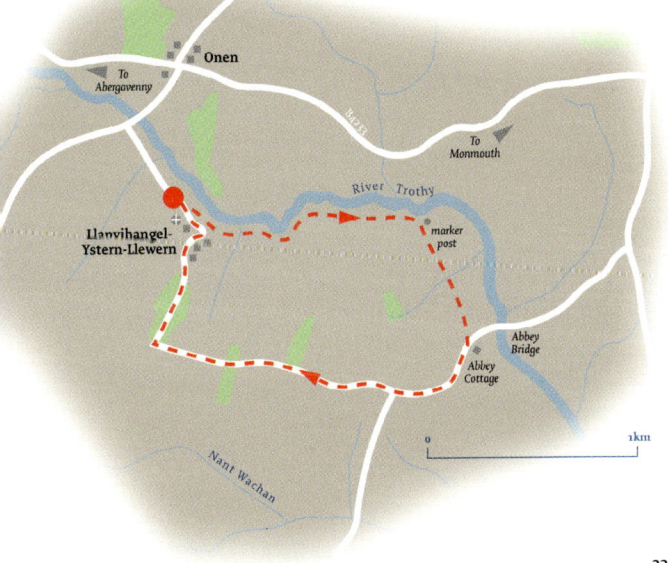

Monmouth and the King's Wood

Distance 6km **Time** 2 hours **Terrain** lanes, fields and woods **Map** OS Explorer OL14 **Access** buses to Monmouth from Chepstow, Hereford and Ross

Stride out and enjoy the high ground above Monmouth before exploring one of the most historic market towns in Britain.

Just before the River Monnow enters the Wye at Monmouth, it arcs a great bow. On the higher ground enclosed by this meander are the remains of the Norman castle, and a millennium before that the Romans had sited their military camp of Blestium here.

The walk starts from the lower end of Monnow Street at the Monnow Bridge over the River Monnow. Its 13th-century fortified gatehouse, the only surviving one in Britain, is one of the iconic features of the lower Wye Valley and gives a good viewpoint back over the town. Vehicles were able to pass through the central arch until just a few years ago, but access has been improved, if not the view, by the addition of a steel and concrete bridge a little downstream. It is one of four gates into the town and before the current stone structure there was a wooden bridge here – its remains were dated by tree-ring analysis to the 1170s. The south side of the bridge marks the boundary with Overmonnow, known as Cappers Town as it was the centre for the making of the famous Monmouth caps. Headgear does not carry the same significance today, but more familiar are the muntlings – a type of street-skirmishing in which gangs of youths from Cappers Town met the Up-Town boys for fisticuffs on the bridge at the end of May. There was a return fixture sometime in June.

MONMOUTH AND THE KING'S WOOD

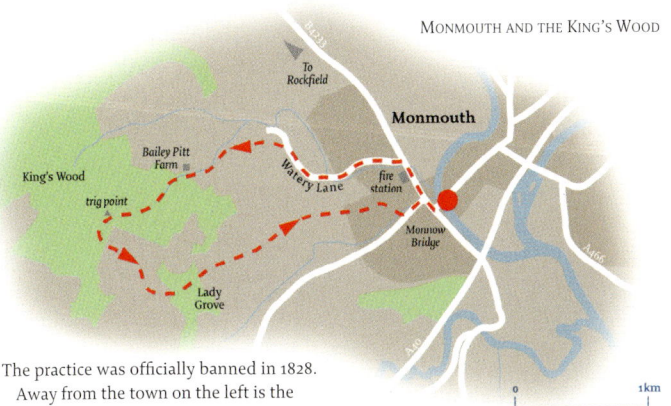

The practice was officially banned in 1828.

Away from the town on the left is the old red sandstone church of St Thomas. Turn right along Drybridge Street and pass in front of Drybridge House along Rockfield Road. Just past the fire station, look out on the left for Watery Lane and follow the route of Offa's Dyke Path which soon bears to the left away from the new housing estate. The lane narrows and, soon after it bends right, go left through the open entrance to a large field, and then pass under electricity lines across the field to the buildings of Bailey Pitt Farm (if crops block the way, use the field edge next to the lane a little further on). At the former farm, cross onto the lane and turn left to pass between the hedge, with its small stream, and the buildings.

At the top of the garden, the path enters King's Wood and becomes a bridleway, which climbs up through the mixed woodland. On reaching a second forestry track, turn left round the bend and take the next track on the left, which soon levels out and contours the hill's eastern slopes through Hunt Grove, with widening views of the Wye Valley below. The very top of the hill and its triangulation pillar can be reached via a short detour up to the right.

After the track bends right on the south side of the hill, turn sharp left downhill onto a bridleway to reach the edge of the woodland at a pair of gates. Here, a double line of mature oak trees leads to the bottom of the field and, hidden on the left, a stile into Lady Grove Wood. A pleasant woodland track descends to the edge of the wood. Here, cross into a field and along the fence to a double stile down into the next field. From here, you can use the spire of St Mary's Church in Monmouth as a guide over a series of fields downhill, tracking a little to the left as the ground levels out, and in just over 1km you reach the outskirts of Monmouth. Pass under electricity lines and then between buildings and finally houses. The path keeps to the right of the former grounds of Drybridge House and emerges onto Wonastow Road. Here, turn left and then right to return to Monnow Street.

◀ The Monnow Bridge at Monmouth

Dingestow and the Trothy

Distance 4km **Time** 1 hour 30
Terrain fields and woodland
Map OS Explorer OL14 **Access** buses to Dingestow from Monmouth, Abergavenny and Newport

Wander along the water meadows and up the slopes of the Trothy Valley – a great family walk with lots to see and explore.

The delightful village of Dingestow is set amongst the meadows of the River Trothy, just above the point where the river turns eastwards on its approach to Monmouth and the Wye. To the northeast there is high ground, which gives a commanding viewpoint deeper into Wales.

From the centre of the village, pass Bridge Farm and Salter's Cottage and turn right along the lane past the parish church, which is dedicated to St Dingat. This is one of only three dedications to the Celtic saint and tradition has it that he is buried here. The list of vicars goes back to 1390 and the remains of Dingestow Castle a little further down the lane have been dated to 1182, when the timber buildings were burnt down. The tump of the castle is accessible to the public through a gateway on the left.

Just beyond the tump, take the footpath on the right into the fields to the west of the Trothy. Head north for 1km over five fields, with the river never far away on the

◀ In the fields above Dingestow

right (halfway through the third field, bear a little left away from the river to find the stile). The area is prone to flooding, but in good weather during spring and summer there is very pleasant walking here. At the top of the fifth field, with the buildings of Lower Llantrothy away on the left, cross the Trothy on a footbridge beneath a large oak tree.

Now turn sharp right for a short way along the river and, where it bends south, head up the slope ahead to a gate into the field beyond. Cross diagonally to the top of this field and go through a gate onto a track which leads through Treowen Wood, where it is often possible to surprise fallow deer. In 300m, at a track junction, turn right and approach the rear of Treowen House, with good views to the south and west. The house today is one of the most impressive private houses in Monmouthshire. When it was built in the early 1600s, of pink old red sandstone, its height and design must have been imposing, set as it is on the high ground overlooking the Trothy Valley.

Pass the main house and, just beyond the last buildings, turn right off the driveway to the house through a gate and across two fields to descend to Mill Wood. Head down on a clear path through the wood. Just above the road, on the right, is a mound, the remains of a motte and bailey, and well worth exploring, as are the small dells on the other side of the path. At the road, turn right over a bridge across the Trothy to return to Dingestow.

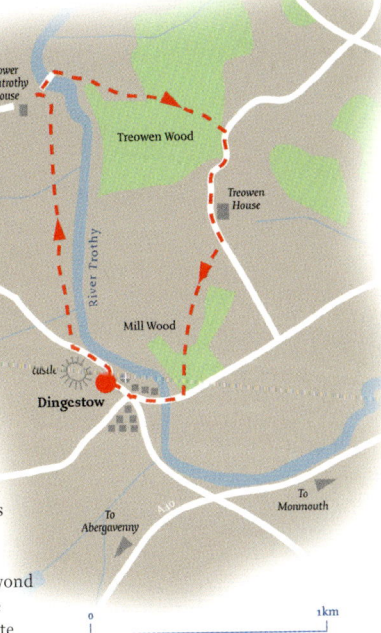

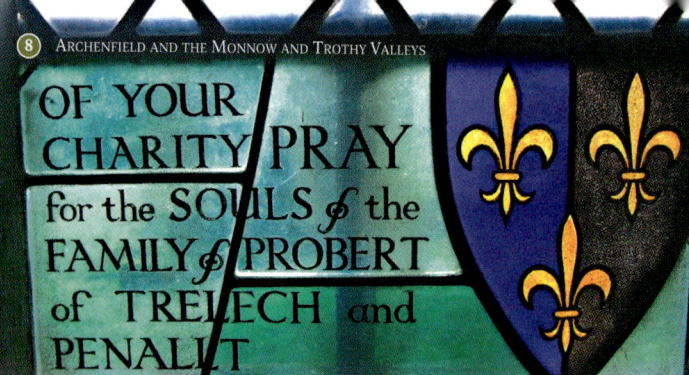

The lost treasures of Troy

Distance 8km **Time** 2 hours 30
Terrain fields, woodland paths and lanes
Map OS Explorer OL14 **Access** buses to
Monmouth from Chepstow, Hereford
and Ross-on-Wye

**Climb the high ground to the south of
Monmouth for extensive views before
reaching the hidden settlement of
Penallt perched on the hillside above
the Wye Valley.**

From the old Monnow Bridge with its
gatehouse, follow the line of the River
Monnow along Cinderhill Street, past the
new bridge, under the dual carriageway
and up to the Mitchell Troy road (B4293).
Turn left along the pavement, and at the
bend bear left down the track to Troy
Farm. Just beyond a bridge over the River
Trothy, which flows into the Wye a little
further on, pass Troy House.

The north front's unusual number of
storeys (three rather than two), 13 bays
and double flight of steps give it an
imposing look. It was built in the 1680s
at a cost of £3000 by the first Duke of
Beaufort as a second home for his son
once he married, their main residence in
Monmouth being Great Castle House,
built only the previous decade. For much
of the 20th century, the nuns of the Order
of the Good Shepherd ran the place as a
school for errant girls.

At the rear of the farm, a sunken track
leads uphill into fields. In the second field
bear diagonally left up to a stile into
woodland, with a great view scanning
west to east over the Trothy Valley and in
the distance the Black Mountains, the
King's Wood, and the hills above Garway,
with the valley of the Monnow in the
centre, then the Buckholt stretching
northwards, the high ground of Welsh
Newton Common, and, curling round the
foot of the Kymin, the River Wye. The
route bears left and then right – look out

The Lost Treasures of Troy

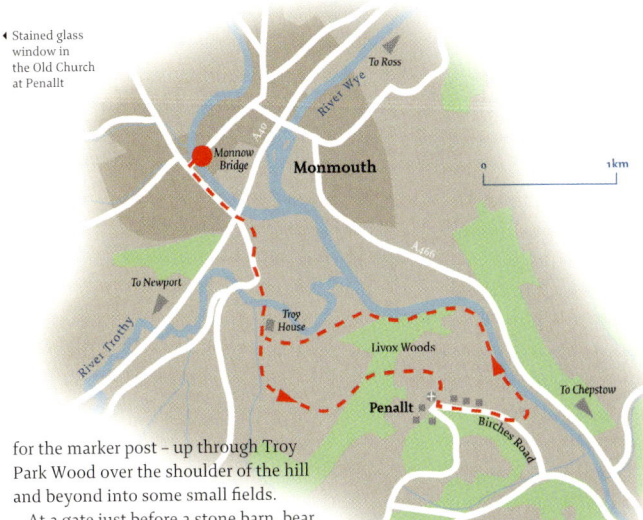

◀ Stained glass window in the Old Church at Penallt

for the marker post – up through Troy Park Wood over the shoulder of the hill and beyond into some small fields.

At a gate just before a stone barn, bear left down to Penallt Church. This is the village's old church, unusual in having no known dedication, and is set in a lofty position above the Wye Valley, though the size of the graveyard hints that it was not always so isolated a place. Inside, on the west wall, hangs the royal coat of arms of Queen Anne with the motto 'semper eadem' (always the same); originally it was hung facing the congregation, an imposing reminder of the political power of the monarch, then recently demonstrated in the 1707 Act of Union of England and Scotland; or perhaps more accurately it was an Act which linked Scotland with the 1536 Union of England and Wales. There is also a strange diagonal passageway and arch from the aisle to the chancel.

Beyond the lych gate, look out for an old chestnut tree (the village stocks were located here) and, opposite, a stone mounting block. The route turns left here down Birches Road for just under 500m and then bears left, past the entrance to Hillside Farm, onto a sunken track (look out for the marker on the telegraph pole). The track weaves its way down through Washing's Wood to the River Wye.

Now follow the bank upstream and along the edge of Livox Wood, passing the remains of a series of small weirs before emerging onto the flood meadows. Nearing the Trothy once more, climb the small knoll ahead to a track, which leads back to Troy Farm and the outward route.

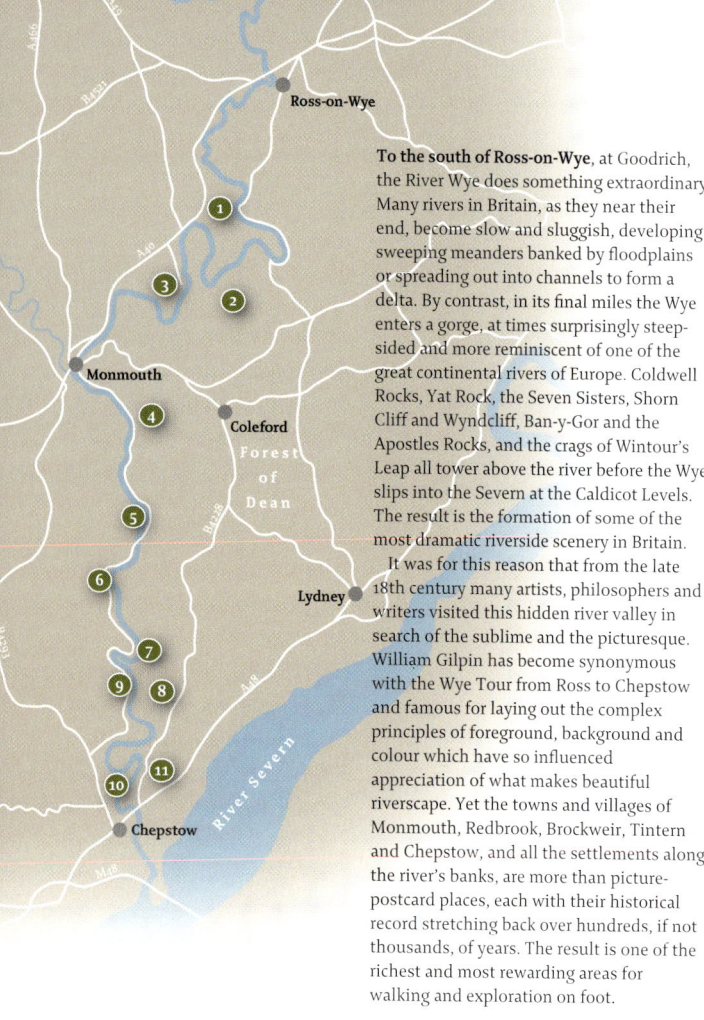

To the south of Ross-on-Wye, at Goodrich, the River Wye does something extraordinary. Many rivers in Britain, as they near their end, become slow and sluggish, developing sweeping meanders banked by floodplains or spreading out into channels to form a delta. By contrast, in its final miles the Wye enters a gorge, at times surprisingly steep-sided and more reminiscent of one of the great continental rivers of Europe. Coldwell Rocks, Yat Rock, the Seven Sisters, Shorn Cliff and Wyndcliff, Ban-y-Gor and the Apostles Rocks, and the crags of Wintour's Leap all tower above the river before the Wye slips into the Severn at the Caldicot Levels. The result is the formation of some of the most dramatic riverside scenery in Britain.

It was for this reason that from the late 18th century many artists, philosophers and writers visited this hidden river valley in search of the sublime and the picturesque. William Gilpin has become synonymous with the Wye Tour from Ross to Chepstow and famous for laying out the complex principles of foreground, background and colour which have so influenced appreciation of what makes beautiful riverscape. Yet the towns and villages of Monmouth, Redbrook, Brockweir, Tintern and Chepstow, and all the settlements along the river's banks, are more than picture-postcard places, each with their historical record stretching back over hundreds, if not thousands, of years. The result is one of the richest and most rewarding areas for walking and exploration on foot.

Cliffs of the River Wye at Chepstow ▶

The Wye Gorge

1. **Coppet Hill and Coldwell Rocks** 42
   A bit of puff is needed at the start, but the rewards are worth it on this classic round

2. **English Bicknor and Offa's Dyke** 44
   There's plenty to see on this route and the riverbank is an ideal place for a picnic or a dip

3. **King Arthur's Cave and the Seven Sisters** 46
   Don't forget to pack a torch on this classic route above the Wye Gorge

4. **Redbrook and the Newland meander** 48
   A river runs through it, or used to, on this ancient round

5. **The mills of Whitebrook** 50
   Two hidden valleys full of delight and history

6. **Cleddon Falls and Catbrook** 52
   See the waterfall from above, then wander through a walled fieldscape

7. **Brockweir and The Hudnalls** 54
   Enter the former world of charcoal burners and smallholders on these steep slopes above the Wye

8. **The Devil's Pulpit from Brockweir** 56
   Make the longer walk to this famous viewpoint

9. **The Eagle's Nest and Tintern** 58
   Counting the steps to this viewpoint will leave you tempted to continue to the ruins of Tintern Abbey

10. **Chepstow Castle to Piercefield** 60
    Follow many a Wye tourist and see the bygone landscape of the lower Wye

11. **The cliffs of Lancaut** 62
    Scramble on the path between river and cliff to find a secluded chapel

Coppet Hill and Coldwell Rocks

Distance 12km **Time** 3 hours 30
Terrain lanes and riverside paths, with steep slopes on Coppet Hill
Map OS Explorer OL14 **Access** buses to Goodrich from Ross and Monmouth

Hill and riverside combine to make this the perfect half-day walk – or take a picnic and make a lazy day of it.

Perched on high ground between sweeping loops of the River Wye, Goodrich marks a significant change in the landscape of the Wye Valley. From the relatively flat and lazy lowlands upstream, the river now twists and turns before entering a gorge-like riverscape past Coldwell Rocks on its way to Symonds Yat and the cliffs of the Seven Sisters. For good reason the Romans named it *Vaga*, 'the Wanderer'.

One of the main attractions of Goodrich is the castle, just to the north of the village centre where parking is available. From the bus stop at the bottom of Castle Lane, take the minor road to Courtfield and Welsh Bicknor uphill over the B4229 towards Coppet Hill. After 500m you reach a fork in the road. Here, look out for the path between the forks, up steps through woodland and past outcrops of pudding stone rocks – you can clearly see pebbles embedded in the rock. Climb fairly steeply to emerge from the woods onto the well-defined north ridge which leads to a triangulation point and the base of a stone folly just beyond. The views from here on a clear day are a just reward for the effort of ascent.

Descend Coppet Hill's long south ridge for 2.5km into woods beside a collapsed drystone wall to reach fields beside the River Wye, opposite the base of Coldwell Rocks. This provides a good spot to rest and watch the peregrine falcons which breed high up on the cliffs. They have now become a tourist attraction in their own right and their presence is protected by the RSPB, though this traditional breeding site nearly saw the last of the falcons in the 1960s because

COPPET HILL AND COLDWELL ROCKS

◀ The River Wye above Coldwell Rocks

of the effects of pesticide poisoning.

The route now turns left to follow the riverside path upstream over fields and through woods to reach Welsh Bicknor in 3km, along what must be one of the most tranquil and idyllic stretches of river the Wye Valley has to offer. A little before Welsh Bicknor the former Monmouth to Ross railway crosses the river from Lydbrook Junction before disappearing into a tunnel under the hill – look out for the pillbox on the left here. (By crossing over the river at this point, the English Bicknor walk, page 44, can be joined.)

Just past the hostel there is a fine Victorian restoration of the church of St Margaret, which houses a 14th-century tomb with an effigy of Margaret Montacute. Outside there is a plague cross, a reminder that even a secluded spot like this did not escape the harsh realities of rural life. It is curious to note that Welsh Bicknor is in England and sited to the east of English Bicknor which lies across the river up the hill – the result of the vagaries of the Wye and the border.

Follow the riverside path for 1km further until you are opposite Lower Lydbrook. At the apex of the river bend, turn left along the line of an old route uphill to Courtfield House. Here, the path becomes a lane which follows the wall of the house's grounds round to the left. You can glimpse the rear of the 19th-century house, which for centuries was the seat of the Vaughan family. More recently it was a retreat for the monks of the Mill Hill Missionary Society. This society was itself founded by Herbert Vaughan, who became a cardinal of the Roman Catholic Church and was responsible in 1895 for the building of the new Westminster Cathedral. The lane continues along the ridge with broad views back down to the Wye and beyond to the high ground of the Forest of Dean. A little past Courtfield Farm, the lane becomes a pleasant minor road and in just over 2km leads back to Goodrich.

English Bicknor and Offa's Dyke

Distance 6km **Time** 2 hours
Terrain fields, lanes and riverside paths
Map OS Explorer OL14 **Access** buses to English Bicknor from Ross and Monmouth

Step back through history in a place where people have lived and worked the land for the last 6000 years.

English Bicknor is one of the oldest settlements in the area. Today the most visible remains of former times are the Norman church and the moat of the 12th-century motte and bailey castle which still surrounds the church. A hint of even greater antiquity is given by the oval shape of the churchyard, pointing to the presence of Saxon building, and the well-preserved section of Offa's Dyke which runs just below the village. In addition local archaeologists have identified a Roman settlement near the southern edge of the village and flint tools have been found, suggesting Neolithic peoples inhabited the site. It is a great village to explore before or after the walk which begins from the car park near the school, where there is also an excellent information board.

A footpath passes to the left (west) of the school and church, heading north across fields, over the top of the hill to a fence, and right along the field edge to another stile just beyond the roadside house. The route descends NNE between strips of woodland along a broad ridge over three fields. Here the path turns left to reach the top of a lane down to the road and the outskirts of Lower Lydbrook. Turn left onto the road and in 150m round the bend take the public footpath on the

◀ Tombstone in churchyard of St Mary the Virgin at English Bicknor

left to the River Wye and under the disused railway bridge of the former Ross to Monmouth line. (At this point the Coppet Hill walk may be joined by crossing the bridge and turning right.) This is the site of Lydbrook Junction, where the Severn and Wye Railway joined to give access to the coalmines of the Forest of Dean.

Now follow the Wye Valley Walk riverside path downstream for just over 1km, between a picturesque anglers' hut on the left and a launching stage on the right and then over fields. This section by the river is one of the most pleasant riverside stretches and it is possible in various places to get down to the water's edge where there are some small strands, great for seeing the river close up or for cooling off the feet on a hot day. Just beyond a metal kissing gate, where the path enters woodland, leave the Wye Valley Walk and turn left along the disused railway track into a field. Here, the route bears to the right through a well-preserved section of Offa's Dyke, a reminder that the border is not far away and of the strategic importance to the dyke of the Wye.

A bit of puff is now required to climb southwest over fields to a lane. Go left up the lane, in 200m passing a path which leads to the restored Rosemary Topping limekilns. The lane continues uphill to a junction, beyond which a detour can take you to Bicknor Court. To reach English Bicknor, turn left and a last pull uphill brings you back to the village.

King Arthur's Cave and the Seven Sisters

Distance shorter option 1.5km; longer option 6km **Time** 1 hour or 2-3 hours **Terrain** woodland and riverside paths, lanes, cliff edges **Map** OS Explorer OL14 **Access** no public transport to the start

Explore the legendary King Arthur's Cave before following the line of the Seven Sisters, a series of limestone cliffs hanging above the Wye Gorge. There is an option to extend the walk to Symonds Yat (East) with its famous Yat Rock viewpoint and cross the river on a small ferry.

From White Rocks Nature Reserve car park by Doward Park Campsite, walk back down the road past the entrance to the campsite. A little further on take the first track on the left downhill to an old quarry. Here, bear to the right to continue past a line of caves.

The last and largest is King Arthur's Cave with its double entrance and two large chambers. Here, in 1695, a goatherd discovered a large skeleton with the remains of a spear; local legend claims it was the body of King Arthur himself. In 1870 the Rev W S Symonds, one of the founders of the local Woolhope Naturalists' Field Club, unearthed the bones of extinct mammals, including mammoths and cave lions, which may well have been gnawed by hyenas, along with flint implements of Palaeolithic people and Neolithic pottery, so adding to the evidence establishing the antiquity of humankind. He also found rolled river pebbles, which could only have been introduced by a river flowing 90m above the present bed of the Wye.

Rejoin the path which soon curves to the left and descends gently until a small band of limestone rocks appears on the left. Bear left up through the rocks and along the top of the Seven Sisters cliff. Short side-paths lead to the cliff edges where there are sheer drops from the top of the limestone rock towers, on which rare species associated with natural

KING ARTHUR'S CAVE AND THE SEVEN SISTERS

◀ Hand-pull ferry at Symonds Yat

grassland grow, and views along one of the finest river gorges in southern Britain.

A little further on, in a dip, a path leads off left uphill. The shorter option follows this path, soon passing the disused White Rocks quarry before joining a forest track up to Doward Park Campsite.

To take the longer option to Symonds Yat, cross the dip and climb through a second band of rocks until a wide forest track is reached. Turn right downhill to the Biblins Campsite. Now cross the suspension bridge and turn left on a riverside track to reach the hotels and houses of Symonds Yat just beyond a run of rapids. From here, by a series of steps, Yat Rock can be reached, and peregrine falcons, goshawks and buzzards frequently spotted. Recross the river by the hand-pull ferry, for which there is a small charge. (If the river is in flood or to avoid the ferry crossing, do not cross Biblins Bridge but follow a riverside path on the Biblins side to reach the bank opposite Symonds Yat.)

From the bank opposite Symonds Yat, turn left and follow the twisting lane ahead uphill and, just before a postbox, turn left again up an easily-missed path between houses to meet a woodland track. Bear left, soon passing an old quarry with a small memorial stone on the right. Continue to climb, and take the next path right uphill to soon pass a cave on the right. Just beyond, as the path levels out in front of a fenced-off area of cave entrances, turn right. Follow this track and its fence uphill as it curves to the left, ignoring two other paths forking right. The track soon levels off, with open woodland on the left and an old drystone wall boundary on the right. At a crosspaths, continue straight ahead. The track soon becomes a lane to take you back to Doward Park Campsite.

47

Redbrook and the Newland meander

Distance 7km **Time** 2 hours **Terrain** tracks and lanes **Map** OS Explorer OL14
Access buses to Redbrook from Monmouth and Chepstow

A climb through woods from riverside Redbrook leads to the picturesque village of Newland, with its impressive church known as the Cathedral of the Forest, before retracing the route of an ancient meander of the River Wye.

The walk starts opposite the car park and small recreation area at the Village Stores. Take the rising lane to the left and bear right in front of the school. Follow the lane uphill and enter woodland where the lane becomes a track. As the track levels out, bear right onto an old tramroad track.

The wood here is called Forge Wood – a reminder that Redbrook was an important industrial centre for smelting iron ore, for which large amounts of charcoal were needed. It is possible to see the remains of charcoal and other workings in the woods off the path. Continue ahead, ignoring paths off right, to the top of the slope to emerge from the woods.

Bear left and follow the track in a tree-lined holloway downhill to the outskirts of Newland, to a sign off right for a restricted byway (this is the start of the return route). To enter Newland village, continue ahead and take the first lane on the left up Savage Hill to the village centre and its All Saints Church. The church, dating back to the 13th century, is known locally as the Cathedral of the

Redbrook and the Newland meander

Forest because of its size and setting. Inside are a number of effigies and monuments, including the Miner's Brass engraving. To the west of the church is the former grammar school and to the south is a row of almshouses established by the benefactor William Jones, a member of the Haberdashers' Livery Company.

To start the return, retrace steps to the restricted byway sign. Turn left along this lane, which soon turns into a track as the view opens out. On the left is the distinctive shape of a V-shaped river valley. Here the ancient Newland meander can be seen as it curves around to the right with remnants of old woodland on the slopes above. It is thought that the Wye once followed this course at a height 90m above its current level. Continue until you cross a small stone bridge over Valley Brook just before the buildings of Lodges Farm.

Follow the byway as it now turns right, off the track, over fields with Valley Brook below on the right. The byway curves right to Birt's Cottage and then starts the descent to recross Valley Brook at a drystone-walled bridge. Go past two large ponds to the point where the byway descends left. Leave the byway and take the right fork ahead along a wide footpath.

In the past the descent to Redbrook would have been very different, with clouds of smoke rising and the noise of industrial activity, most recently from the trains of the Wye Valley Railway which ran from Monmouth to Chepstow from 1876 to 1964, or from the Tinplate Works which only ceased production in 1962. These had succeeded the Copper Works at the start of the 18th century, when copper ore was shipped from Cornwall and up the Wye from Chepstow to the quayside in Redbrook – The Boat Inn across the old railway bridge serves as a reminder of the past reliance on river transportation. The woodlands on either side of Valley Brook would have been dotted with the small cottages and huts of charcoal burners whose livelihood depended on supplying fuel for the furnaces. A little way down, the path again crosses Valley Brook and becomes a lane which leads back into Redbrook.

◀ Newland All Saints Church, the Cathedral of the Forest

The mills of Whitebrook

Distance 4km **Time** 1 hour 30
Terrain some steep paths and tracks with 170m of ascent **Map** OS Explorer OL14
Access buses from Chepstow and Monmouth via Trellech stop at The Narth

Discover the Wye Valley's industrial past among the ruins of two now secluded and peaceful tributaries.

The White Brook flows from the high ground around Trellech and quickly plunges through a steep-sided wooded gorge which can only be glimpsed from the River Wye below. Now the valley is a tranquil spot full of delightful cottages and bubbling streams. Yet there are many hints of its less picturesque past. Virtually every house is connected in some way to the water-powered industries that became established here from the start of the 17th century, when a branch of Tintern Wireworks was established. A century later, papermaking was flourishing and dotted around are dams, ponds and leats, all connected to the mills and warehouses. However, it was not to last and by 1880 the boom was over.

Today the valley is filled with greenery-

covered ruins and restored private houses clustered around the narrow road which climbs steeply up the valley – there is some roadside parking at the top end of the village. Start the walk a little above the chapel in the middle of the village, and across the White Brook take the track left into Pwllplythin Wood, passing old mill houses and the site of the former Clearwater Paper Mills with its octagonal stone chimney. This was the first paper mill in the valley, dating from 1760, and was even fitted with a steam engine in the 1860s.

The track climbs gently through woods with the brook down on the left. Shortly after the track crosses the brook, it meets the road. Turn right and after 100m, just before the next house, turn sharp left uphill on a footpath. This old route, lined with drystone walls, climbs steeply through woodland to The Narth (ignore a footpath left after the path levels out). Now turn left along the road into the centre of The Narth.

Just round the right-hand bend, in the centre of the village, take a path on the left to Manorside. Descend gently, over a crosspaths, to a metal kissing gate. Turn left and almost immediately right to continue the descent through woodland to a forest track and Manor Brook. Cross the brook and pick a way up the far bank to reach another forest track. Here, turn left and follow the brook downhill. After 200m, just beyond a prominent path branching right uphill, leave the track and take the signed path off left to continue downhill. Follow this path, which can be wet after rain, with Manor Brook down on the left, until you reach a house. Here, the path becomes a track and soon arrives at a lane. Now turn left downhill to reach the centre of Whitebrook.

Octagonal chimney of the former Clearwater Paper Mills at Whitebrook

Cleddon Falls and Catbrook

Distance 5km **Time** 1 hour 30
Terrain woodland, fields and lanes
Map OS Explorer OL14 **Access** buses from Monmouth and Chepstow stop at Llandogo, where there is a steep signed route to the top of Cleddon Falls

Take life slowly and enjoy the woods, views and waterfalls above Llandogo.

This makes for an ideal family outing. Just off the Tintern to Trellech road above Llandogo, the car park at Whitestone (GR525029) at the southern end of Bargain Wood is a great place for a picnic and for children of all ages to run around. There is also a small play area with some wooden climbing frames and posts.

Follow the Wye Valley Walk path northwards on a broad track through Bargain Wood, past three viewpoints, each one giving a slightly different perspective down to the Wye Valley. The woodland is a delight at any time of year, but is perhaps at its best in early spring or the leaf-fall of autumn. Its name is something of a misnomer and is thought to be a corruption of 'bare gain', referring derogatorily to the poor grazing to be had here in former times, but there's plenty of scope for exploring off the path here.

Where the track bends sharp left, bear right, still on the Wye Valley Walk, and soon descend between moss-covered boundary walls to the houses of Cleddon and its falls. The approach from Llandogo requires a steep climb of over 150m through the woods, but on this route you arrive at the top of the falls, where the stream leaves the gently sloping plateau.

The point at which this stream, and many others in the valley, suddenly plunge down marks what may have been the level of an ancient sea, before the

Cleddon Falls and Catbrook

◀ Cleddon Falls above Llandogo

passing of successive ice ages caused sea levels to drop and the course of the Wye to become entrenched in the gorge we see today. It is possible to descend right, with care, down steps to gain a clearer view of the falls.

Just beyond, at the road, leave the Wye Valley Walk path and turn left with Cleddon Hall soon visible on the right, where the philosopher Bertrand Russell was born, and after 500m, at a crossroads, turn left to a junction, passing the lower end of Cleddon Bog. If time and footwear allow, the bog is worth exploring, though it is a sensitive site, being the largest surviving area of heath that used to cover much of the Trellech plateau.

To continue, cross the road, dog-legging left then right onto a track into Ninewells Wood – now much of it is conifer plantation but the wells around its perimeter are still there. Go uphill round the right bend and in 200m turn left onto a crosspath. In 100m fork left and soon reach the edge of the woodland.

The landscape now takes on a sudden change, with many of the field boundaries made of drystone walling, and even the stiles are of stone, giving the area a feel similar to that of the southern part of the Peak District. Cross a stone stile and follow the drystone wall on the left over two fields with views ahead to the Severn Estuary. In the third field, go diagonally right and cross the next to the corner of the copse ahead. Descend southwest through the wood and the small fields beyond to Catbrook. Here, a left turn downhill along the road for 1km makes for pleasant walking. Finally, bear right at the junction which is just a short distance above the turning to Whitestone car park.

Brockweir and The Hudnalls

Distance 6km **Time** 2 hours
Terrain byways, woodland and riverside paths; ascent of 200m
Map OS Explorer OL14 **Access** buses from Monmouth and Chepstow stop on the A466 opposite Brockweir

Follow the twisting lanes made by woodland squatters as you ascend St Briavels Common and walk in the footsteps of former bargemen beside the River Wye.

The former riverside port of Brockweir lies on the Gloucestershire side of the River Wye and, until the current bridge was built at the start of the 20th century, the crossing had to be made by ferry. At one time the village had over a dozen inns and drinking houses to meet the demand of all the shipbuilders and workers. The barge-trade was the main business here in the 19th century and it would have been a common sight to see teams of men in harness pulling flat-bottomed barges laden with coal or iron upstream to Monmouth and even as far as Hereford. It can be a popular place for summer tourists and there is some parking near the top end of the village; alternatively park in the lay-by on the A466 and walk over the bridge.

Just beyond the bridge over the River Wye, turn left along Underhill Road. Pass a turning off left and a footpath off right and, 100m beyond, turn right just before Orchard Cottage onto a restricted byway which leads uphill in a northerly direction through an area known as The Hudnalls. In origin this was common woodland and an outlier of the Forest of Dean. It was long used for both coppicing and as wood pasture for grazing animals.

◀ The River Wye and the old quayside at Brockweir

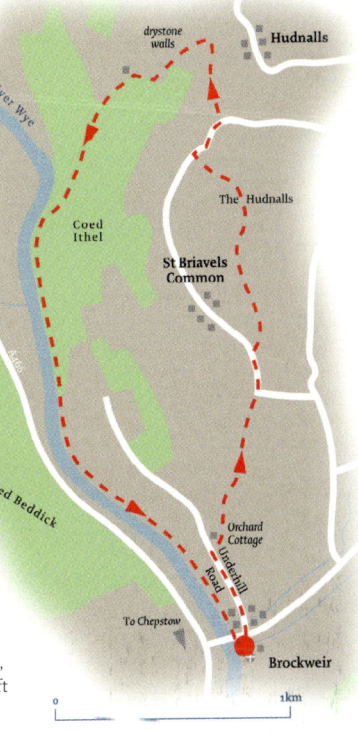

However, in the 19th century the common was gradually occupied by squatters who built small cottages and enclosed the land in small fields. It is this pattern of settlement which is still visible today and accounts for many of the winding paths and lanes.

At the first lane, dog-leg right, then left and 250m further on, at a second lane, turn right and head round the left bend to pick up a sign for Offa's Dyke Path (ODP) which is now followed for the next 1.5km and soon turns right off the lane up over the brow of St Briavels Common. The route now descends over two fields in a northwesterly direction and turns right along the lane for 200m. At this point, look out for the waymark indicating a left turn off the lane and onto a byway.

Proceed along the byway for 350m and, at the end of the field on the left, turn left off ODP. Take the byway downhill, ignoring paths off right. The wide path descends round to the left through woodland, flanked initially by drystone walls, and soon turns right down zigzags to a crosspaths just before a house. Here turn left downhill, a little steeply at first, and then bear further round to the left, still heading down through the woodland.

Soon the River Wye can be glimpsed on the right through the trees. The path emerges from the woods by the river just below Coed Ithel weir, which marks the limit of the tidal stream. Now turn left and follow the pleasant riverside path downstream. Just before reaching Brockweir Bridge you pass the old quayside, where the boats known as Severn Trows docked, having navigated the waters from Chepstow, in order to have their goods transferred into shallower barges for the onward journey.

The Devil's Pulpit from Brockweir

Distance 7km **Time** 2 hours 30
Terrain lanes, fields and wooded slopes; with 200m of ascent **Map** OS Explorer OL14
Access buses from Monmouth and Chepstow stop on the A466 over the River Wye ffrom Brockweir

Forget the direct route from Tintern – it's a devil of a path – and follow the lie of the land to reach one of the iconic viewpoints in the lower Wye Valley.

The Devil's Pulpit is rightly one of the most visited natural attractions in the lower Wye Valley. The most direct and popular route crosses the river at Tintern and climbs the steep slope which lower down the valley forms the rocky outcrop of Shorn Cliff, the haunt of climbers and nesting birds. A start from Brockweir allows a more leisurely ascent and also the chance to see a well-preserved section of Offa's Dyke. Brockweir is now a quiet riverside village, worth exploring in its own right.

Take the lane by the Malt House and the 14th-century Monks Hall and, soon after, turn left onto the route of Offa's Dyke Path (ODP). Continue uphill above a small valley, bearing round to the south and ignoring the route off left to Madgett Hill. Cross a stile into a field and bear slightly right, keeping to the line of ODP up to and through a strip of woodland and the dyke itself.

This makes a good spot to pause and take in the view – to the west is the

The Devil's Pulpit from Brockweir

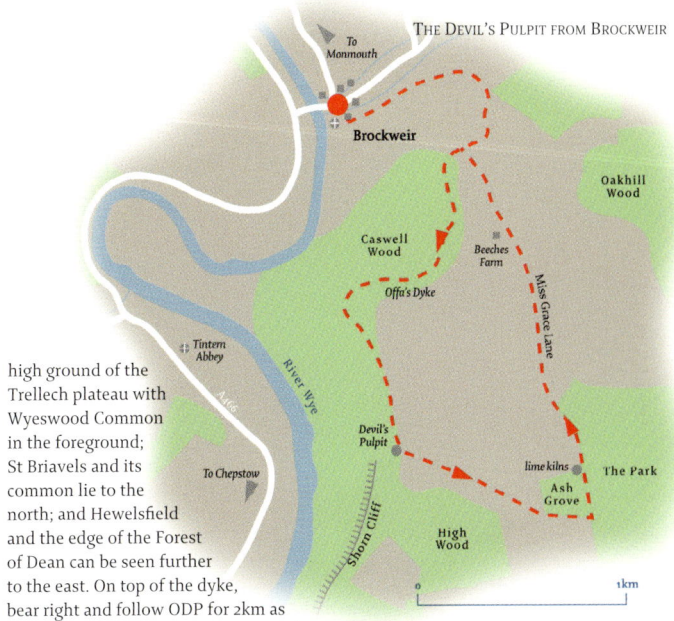

high ground of the Trellech plateau with Wyeswood Common in the foreground; St Briavels and its common lie to the north; and Hewelsfield and the edge of the Forest of Dean can be seen further to the east. On top of the dyke, bear right and follow ODP for 2km as it meanders south and west up through woods along the line of the dyke itself. Pass a metal kissing gate on the left and shortly beyond reach the Devil's Pulpit rock with its famous view down to Tintern Abbey.

In one version of the fanciful story, the devil gave up haranguing the Cistercians below to abandon their devotional life and descended from his airy rock to the abbey itself, suggesting he preach a sermon to them from a more conventional pulpit. The monks agreed but Old Nick was outwitted inside when he was showered with holy water, which sent him off towards Llandogo with his tail firmly between his legs.

Retrace steps to the metal kissing gate and turn right through it, off ODP, and across four fields with views opening out over the Severn Estuary (follow the hedge on the left in the first field, go diagonally right across the second and third to the corner of a wood, and keep the wood on the left in the fourth) to reach Miss Grace Lane. Turn left along the lane for 1.5km, passing old limekilns on the left after 300m, to Beeches Farm. Pass to the right of the farm buildings across the lawn of the campsite. Now descend northwest over three fields to reach the outward route on Offa's Dyke Path once again and retrace steps downhill for 1km to Brockweir.

◂ Above Brockweir looking north to St Briavels Common

The Eagle's Nest and Tintern

Distance 1.5km (or 8km) **Time** 1 hour (or 3 hours) **Terrain** woodland, fields and lanes, with some steep paths and cliff edges **Map** OS Explorer OL14 **Access** buses from Monmouth and Chepstow stop just east of Lower Wyndcliff car park

Take in the best viewpoint in the Wye Valley with an option to extend the walk and follow in the footsteps of the medieval monks of Tintern.

The Eagle's Nest viewpoint was created in 1828 for the Duke of Beaufort as part of the Piercefield Park Picturesque Walks, designed in the 18th century by Valentine Morris the Younger, with the 365 Steps as the culmination of the walk. Lower Wyndcliff car park on the A466 between Tintern and St Arvans has plenty of parking, some picnic tables and a useful information board.

Take the path (signposted for the 365 Steps) across the road from the car park into woodland dominated by yew and beech. In 100m bear right in front of a small limestone cliff and soon start the 100m ascent of the Wyndcliff on a meandering path up rough steps, with views out over the Wye Gorge and beyond to the Severn Estuary. Near the top, as the path levels out, turn right at a junction onto the Wye Valley Walk path and in 150m come to the Eagle's Nest viewpoint down on the right.

For the shorter route return back down the Wye Valley Walk to Upper Wyndcliff car park and then left down through woodland to the start. For the longer option to Tintern, head northwards on the Wye Valley Walk for 1.5km along the top of Black Cliff Wood to the prominent earthworks of a hillfort. Here, the path

THE EAGLE'S NEST AND TINTERN

◀ The ruins of Tintern Abbey

descends steeply on the right. Below the fort, bear right for 100m, then left down to a stile. Here, leave the Wye Valley Walk and bear right (northeast) down three fields, past Reddings Farm on the right. At the far corner of the third field go through a gate, then immediately left over a stile into woodland, past an old quarry on the left, to a sunken track which leads down to Tintern with its abbey, shops and eateries.

To continue, retrace steps uphill, south along the Wye Valley Walk, past the left turn to Reddings Farm. This is the old medieval route from Tintern to St Arvans – the modern road along the valley was only built in 1824 – and perhaps still gives a hint of the seclusion the Cistercians originally sought in siting their abbey at Tintern. Look out for small tufa beds in the stream on the left as the way climbs to Penterry Lane (ignore the Wye Valley Walk's left turn across the stream). As the route levels out, it is prone to be overgrown – look out for a sturdy stick for some nettle-bashing or in high summer be prepared to escape right on the right of way which heads west to Penterry Lane.

At the lane, bear left and in 400m again turn left, up the driveway to Porthcasseg, whose name means 'mare's gate' and recalls its former role as a staging post for horses. Pass to the rear of the buildings and follow the path to the right between barns onto a field-track heading south. Pass over the brow of the hill and descend past some old limekilns on the left to Upper Wyndcliff car park, with views ahead to the Severn Estuary. At the rear of the car park, take the path on the right down through the woods, bearing left at the bottom of the slope to arrive at the small limestone cliff just up from the A466. Here, turn right down to the road and the start.

Chepstow Castle to Piercefield

Distance 6km **Time** 2 hours **Terrain** woods and parkland **Map** OS Explorer OL14 **Access** buses to Chepstow from Monmouth

From the imposing presence of one of the most magnificent castles in Wales, wander through the 'sublime' landscape of Piercefield Park.

From the mid-18th century, Piercefield Park just north of Chepstow became one of the most sought-after places for those wishing to indulge in the celebration of dramatic landscape scenery. For those embarking on a Wye Tour from Ross, it came to represent the culmination of their journey down the river. The estate was purchased by Valentine Morris and then landscaped by his son, also called Valentine. He created a series of 'sublime' walks along the cliffs, punctuated with features and viewpoints, exploiting the natural topography to its greatest effect.

Start by Chepstow Castle, where there is a car park, and take the surfaced path up Castle Dell past the stone from Plynlimon, which marks the start of the Wye Valley Walk, whose route is followed for the first half of the walk. The castle itself is in a magnificent state of preservation and its towers and walls remain an impressive monument to the Normans who sited this first stone castle in Wales on the last rocky spur of the Wye before it reaches the Severn. The corner tower nearest the car park is Marten's Tower, so named after the republican and regicide Henry Marten, who was imprisoned here by Charles II for 20 years.

At the road, turn right and walk up the hill for 500m to where the route turns right, just before the leisure centre and the comprehensive school. At the rear of the car park, take the path into woodland and pass to the rear of the buildings. In 300m, go through a gap in the boundary wall and turn right down steps a short distance to

CHEPSTOW CASTLE TO PIERCEFIELD

◀ Chepstow Castle

the alcove viewpoint. This is the first of Morris' landscape features and gives a good view downstream to the castle.

Now bear left and follow the route northeastwards through Pierce Wood, past the overgrown platform whose view is now obscured. In just over 500m, the path swings left and then right to cross a dell before zigzagging up through the earthworks of an old hillfort to a now dilapidated grotto on its east side. Beyond the fort, follow the path round to the left and descend gently for 200m to a fork. Here bear left uphill, off the Wye Valley Walk, and soon cross over a stile into Piercefield Park, where the sad remains of Piercefield House stand on the right.

There are many stories associated with the house. Some say its owner is always ill-starred and it's true that Valentine Morris ended his days in poverty and that the second owner, George Smith, spent so much on the place that he bankrupted himself. Others point to American soldiers stationed here in World War II as just one case in its long decline, though their using the house for target practice is perhaps one of those apocryphal wartime stories. Far more engaging is the Spectre of the Mare's Pool, which used to stand by the west wall of the estate. From here on moonlit nights, some believe a ghostly woman rises from the water on the back of a white horse and wings her way northwards over the grounds, always in the direction of Porthcasseg, the Mare's Gate. Quite who this woman is or was or why she travels north is lost to time.

The onward route, however, leads from the house across the parkland to the edge of the racecourse and onto a track which heads south. Pass into the woodland and, after 400m, bear left along the high boundary wall which soon reaches the B4293 above Chepstow. Turn left and once again pass the entrance to the leisure centre and school. From here, retrace steps downhill to the start.

The cliffs of Lancaut

Distance 7km **Time** 2 hours 30
Terrain lanes, field paths and some steeper sections in Lancaut woods
Map OS Explorer OL14 **Access** buses to Chepstow from Monmouth

Experience riverside walking at its best below and above the sheer limestone cliffs of Lancaut.

Chepstow is a border town sited on a bend in the River Wye, just above its confluence with the Severn. The town itself is full of historic buildings and, since well before the Normans arrived, was known as an important crossing point between England and Wales.

The route of the walk passes below and above sheer cliffs used by climbers and the river is tidal with mudflats. There is also one short section of boulder scree to cross.

From Chepstow Castle, walk past the tourist information centre and Chepstow Museum and down to the bridge over the River Wye. This is known as the Old Wye Bridge. Made of cast iron at the start of the 19th century, it was a replacement for a series of timber bridges dating back to medieval times. It gives good views back upstream to the castle and down to the modern road and rail bridges, beyond which are the old wharves of the former port.

On the far side of the bridge, take the lane ahead uphill (signed for the Gloucestershire Way). This is soon joined by Offa's Dyke Path (ODP) from the right, which is now followed northwards. Cross over the B4228 and, in another 150m, ODP bears left into a field beside houses and up between an old look-out tower and Chapelhouse Wood, so named because of the site of a medieval chantry chapel. At the far end of the field, bear right along a

THE CLIFFS OF LANCAUT

◀ Ruins of St James' Church at Lancaut

large wall, then dog-leg left and right between the houses before turning left across a field to reach Lancaut Nature Reserve. Here, leave ODP and bear left into the reserve. The path descends through woodland, with the Wye down on the left and sheer limestone cliffs to the right, from which you are likely to hear the calls of climbers as they test their nerve on routes that range from moderate to extreme.

As the path comes near to the river, there is a short section of boulder scree to cross – for the exact route across, follow the yellow markers and polished rocks. Continue on the riverside path and in another 500m, just before the river bend, pass below Wintour's Leap. The Royalist Sir John Wintour is well-known for his horse's heroic pluck at the time of the Civil War in launching itself down these steep cliffs in order to escape the pursuing Roundheads. Needless to say, Sir John had not endeared himself to the inhabitants of the Forest of Dean – it is said that he had felled all but 200 of the Dean's trees and ensured the forest was staunchly Parliamentarian. Whatever the truth, the impressive cliffs are no place for horseplay.

Round the bend, past the disused Lancaut quarry, is the ruin of St James' Church, once a refuge for lepers. Despite the proximity of Chepstow, the high cliffs of Wintour's Leap and the Apostles Rocks on the Piercefield peninsula opposite still make this a secluded spot. At the church, bear right uphill past a bench and over a metal stile to a path junction just short of some old limekilns. Bear right past the kilns and up to Lancaut Lane. Here, a right turn brings you past the open field of Spital Meend, an Iron Age fort, and just beyond the first house on the right Offa's Dyke itself crosses the lane.

Descend to the road junction and turn right, round the bend, and 150m beyond turn right onto Offa's Dyke Path once more, which follows a line behind the houses along the top of the cliffs. In 500m, the path reaches the road again and bears right, round the bend, before turning off right once more along a walled garden to the entrance to Lancaut Nature Reserve. From here, retrace the outward route.

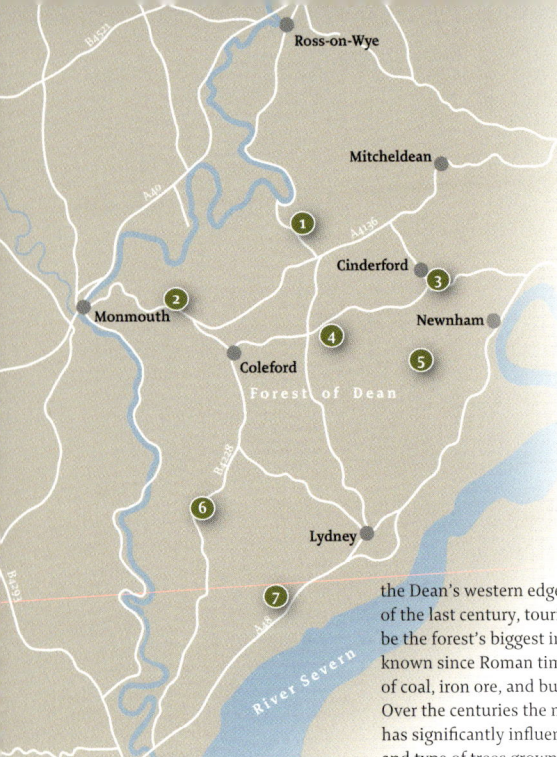

The Royal Forest of Dean is a triangular plateau of woodlands and commons lying between the Severn and Wye Valleys, and in 1938 it was designated England's first National Forest Park, with the towns of Coleford and Cinderford to the north, Lydney and Chepstow in the south, and the ancient administrative centre of St Briavels, now a charming village, on the Dean's western edge. Since the middle of the last century, tourism has grown to be the forest's biggest industry, but it was known since Roman times for the mining of coal, iron ore, and building stone. Over the centuries the need for timber has significantly influenced the number and type of trees grown, from the oaks supplied to royal dockyards since the time of Elizabeth I to the modern plantations of quick-growing conifers favoured in the 20th century. Now, however, the area is undergoing a period of regeneration. The last of the collieries closed in 1965, the Forestry Commission is busy restoring plantations to mixed woodland, and many of the former industrial sites are being sensitively managed for the mutual benefit of residents, visitors and wildlife.

The Forest of Dean

1. Lydbrook and Sallowvallets 66
Wander along the disused railway tracks and through the forest's famous inclosures above this former industrial village

2. The Kymin and the Buckstone 68
Grand views from the Kymin will keep you going on this classic round on the edge of the forest

3. Welshbury Fort and the Dobunni's last stand 70
This is a great little stroll through woodland to an atmospheric hilltop fort with plenty to see and explore

4. Speech House loop 72
A popular spot at the heart of the Forest of Dean, but a delight all the same

5. Soudley Bridge and the Old Dean Road 74
A neat woodland round above this secluded settlement, passing near the Dean Heritage Centre

6. St Briavels and the Slade Brook 76
From the ancient centre of the forest this has it all – a castle, a babbling brook and a vibrant little village

7. Woolaston Ridge and Severn views 78
From the Roman road on the southern slopes of the forest, climb north for great views over the Severn Estuary

Lydbrook and Sallowvallets

Distance 7km **Time** 2 hours **Terrain** forest tracks and paths **Map** OS Explorer OL14 **Access** buses to Lydbrook from Ross-on-Wye and Monmouth

Recall the Forest of Dean's industrial past as you meander along former railway tracks and through woodland plantations.

Lydbrook was one of the major industrial centres of the Forest of Dean. Coal from the nearby mines was brought down to the lower end of the town to be loaded onto barges for onward transportation by barge to Hereford. With the arrival of the railways in the mid 1800s the Severn and Wye Line superseded the river trade and ensured the mining industry continued to flourish for another century. Now tourism has replaced the trains and many of the tracks have been converted for the use of walkers and cyclists. In Lydbrook the Jovial Colliers pub is one of a number of reminders of the area's past. Opposite, set into the imposing wall is a plaque which commemorates the removal by volunteers of the huge coal heap that used to cover what is now the recreation area, where parking is available. Such was the amount of slag dumped here over the decades that it was known as the Blue Mound and must have dominated the entire town.

From here, walk up Church Road and take the first road on the right at the bend, then follow the path on the left up past the churchyard to a gate. Turn right onto the disused railway line and follow it for 1.5km, passing above the spring to Greathough Brook. Just beyond Horton Bridge, at a fork, bear right uphill away from the railway, which soon enters Mirystock Tunnel, on a path which zigzags up to the A4136. Cross the road and take the path on the opposite side which soon descends gently to meet the line of the railway again on the far side of the tunnel, with Mirystock Bridge a little beyond.

Continue for another 1km and, just

◀ Old railway line at Mirystock Bridge

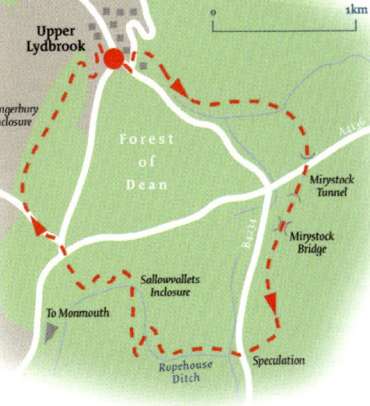

before the main cycle track is joined, turn right, down through Speculation car park, to the road beyond. This is one of a number of former colliery sites which have been given over to the tourist industry – its name perhaps recalls the precarious nature of mining in this area. From here, dog-leg right for 50m, then left across the road on the Wysis Way into woodland. The route follows a rising path westwards alongside Ropehouse Ditch into Sallowvallets Inclosure. Cross over a forestry track and continue along the ditch, whose stream here has been channelled with stone blocks. There are many enclosures in the forest, but Sallowvallets lays claim to being the first place in the area where conifers were planted. The original Weymouth pines, planted in 1781, are long since felled and conservation is now favouring mixed woodland, thereby restoring many areas to the condition envisaged by the 1688 Dean Reafforestation Act.

The Wysis Way now loops north across Ropehouse Ditch and back south before doubling north again for 400m to cross Ropehouse Ditch once more at a crosspaths. Here, turn left for 200m, with the ditch on the left, before bearing to the right and climbing more steeply to a track junction. Turn left round the bend for 250m, where the Wysis Way turns right off the track and almost immediately forks left onto a path, up through a dense conifer plantation for 200m to emerge onto the A4136 again.

Cross the road and, leaving the Wysis Way, dog-leg right and then left down the first lane on the left. Follow the lane for 300m and, just before the brow, bear right onto a woodland path along the western edge of Hangerbury Inclosure. In 250m, the path turns right onto a track between the woodland and fields, heading NNE over Hangerbury Hill with good views west. The path soon descends through woodland and, in another 500m, reaches a lane and the houses above Lydbrook. Cross over the lane and descend between houses, zigzagging more to the right than the left to reach Uphill Road, which brings you back down into Lydbrook a little below the start.

The Kymin and the Buckstone

Distance 8km **Time** 3 hours
Terrain undulating ground in woodland and over fields, with 300m of ascent
Map OS Explorer OL14 **Access** buses to Staunton from Monmouth

Take in the views on a real rollercoaster of a walk on the edge of the Forest of Dean.

The village of Staunton is perched high up on the western edge of the Forest of Dean and for centuries was on one of the main routes into Wales. It still has an impressive church and a welcoming pub, the White Horse Inn.

At the western edge of the village, take the restricted byway northwards. Descend left past St John the Baptist's Well, which now seems rather out of place all on its own. However, a chapel dedicated to St John is recorded in the 14th century, though no trace of it has been found. From here, pick a path straight down the slope through the beech and oak woodland to the forestry track lower down. Turn left uphill onto the route of the Wysis Way (WW), turning right after 250m. The track descends through deciduous woodland to a fork junction. Here, take the left track uphill and look out for a WW sign up left to cross the busy Staunton Road.

Continue on the Wysis Way, but after 300m ignore the next WW sign pointing left across fields and continue into Beaulieu Wood. This woodland was acquired by the Woodland Trust in 2001 – their intention is to restore the mixed broadleaf trees which existed before the area was planted with conifers in the 1950s and which first attracted the Kymin Club, a wealthy group of friends, at the turn of the 19th century to landscape what was then known as Beaulieu Grove with paths and viewing points. After the next left-hand bend, at a slanted crosspaths, turn sharp left uphill.

The path soon bears round to the right on a rising traverse up to outcrops of moss-covered stone, and twists through the outcrops to emerge onto a wooded

THE KYMIN AND THE BUCKSTONE

◀ At the Buckstone looking west

ridge. Follow the path along the ridge, past a viewpoint on the right, to shortly arrive at the Kymin. The top of the hill is dominated by the Round House and the Naval Temple. Nelson had breakfast here in 1802, but it is not recorded whether he enjoyed the magnificent view, which allegedly takes in 10 counties, though he apparently grumbled that the Dean was not planting nearly enough of his 'oaks' to supply the navy. The name of the hill appears to be a corruption of *cae maen*, Welsh for 'stone field', though these have clearly been removed from the lush lawn nearby.

To continue, descend past the Naval Temple and car park to where the Offa's Dyke Path takes you through a metal kissing gate signed for Redbrook. At first, the well-signed path passes through woods and then down across fields, with views of the Wye Valley and Forest of Dean, before joining Duffield's Lane. A little past Duffield's Farm, you come to the line of the former Coleford to Monmouth railway. Here, where the track bends right, take the left fork on a small path, just before a cottage, and descend to the road with a mill pond beyond.

Turn left onto the road and, just after the right bend, take the footpath rising left up to a stile. Here, recross the dismantled railway and bear right uphill, steeply at first, through the woodland of Knockalls Inclosure. At the third forestry track turn left and in 200m bear right past Knockalls Lodge, originally inhabited by a single woodsman who had responsibility for managing the forestry. Round the bend, take the left fork beside a drystone wall up to the dwellings of Buckstone on Staunton Meend.

Pass to the right of the houses, climbing beside a drystone wall to reach the triangulation point through a gate, with the Buckstone itself just to the left. It used to be a logan, but in 1885 a group of travelling actors rocked it off its base and it crashed down the hillside. Somehow it was restored to its original place and, secured by iron and cement, it no longer rocks, though it provides good clambering. To descend to Staunton, continue along the path beside the wall down through the woods.

Welshbury Fort and the Dobunni's last stand

Distance 3km **Time** 1 hour
Terrain woodland tracks and paths
Map OS Explorer OL14 **Access** buses from Coleford stop at Littledean, 1km south of the start point on George Lane

Discover the hidden hillfort of Welshbury, tucked away in woodland on the eastern fringe of the Forest of Dean – an ideal outing for marauding children.

Welshbury hillfort is thought to date from the Iron Age – a Celtic coin and a Roman spearhead have been found here – and the site's occupation may well stretch back to Neolithic times. It is also reputedly the fort where the Dobunni tribe fought their last battle against the Romans. Its detailed history, however, is still shrouded in doubt as the site has never been systematically excavated. What is clear is the system of ditches and ramparts – there is a triple line on the south and west side and a single one on the steeper north and east slopes.

There is a straightforward approach from the edge of the Forestry Commission land (GR672146), 1km north of Littledean along George Lane. From here, walk northeastwards into woodland up a track, passing houses set back on the right, and along the top of Chestnuts Inclosure. In another 200m, where a track comes in from the right, continue ahead and soon arrive at the northern edge of the woodland. Pass through the gate and cross the clearing to the southern edge of Welshbury Wood – there are good views east and west from this spot.

In the wood, bear left onto a path which heads uphill (avoid the track which follows the western edge of the wood) and in 250m pass through the outer

◀ Looking west from near Welshbury Wood

ditches and ramparts of Welshbury Fort.

Continue a little further to the top of the hill, from where the extensive earthworks are clearly visible and can be explored, brambles permitting. The north side, in particular, is fearsomely steep for any attacker and though the whole site is now covered in trees it is still possible to gain an idea of just how commanding a position the fort occupies. Such is the sensitivity of the site that, in order to thin the trees without causing damage to what may lie just below ground level, the owners of the land, the Forestry Commission, reverted to using horses for dragging out the felled timber.

To return, either retrace the outward route or continue a little further to the northern edge of the fort and then bear westwards on a faint path, which initially follows the top of the fortifications, before descending more steeply down the western side of the fort through the series of ramparts and ditches themselves. On reaching the track lower down, turn left and proceed gently uphill to return to the southern edge of the wood and the outward route.

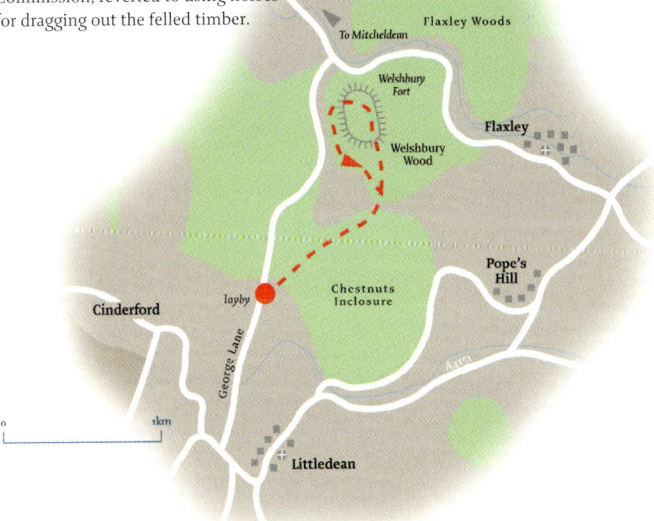

Speech House loop

Distance 6km **Time** 2 hours
Terrain woodland paths and tracks
Map OS Explorer OL14 **Access** buses to Beechenhurst Lodge from Cinderford

Explore the heart of the Forest of Dean and popular Cannop Ponds, before wandering back through Russell's Inclosure.

Beechenhurst Lodge is found right in the centre of the Forest of Dean. It is the former site of Speech House Colliery, though little evidence of the industry remains as the area has been developed for tourists. It makes a good base for a whole day with the family or as a place simply to park before heading off deep into the forest. It can be a popular place in high season, but you don't have to go far to lose the crowds by the café and adventure playground. There are a number of marked routes, including a Sculpture Trail to the rear of the lodge. This walk covers the ground to the south.

Start at the far lower corner of the car park at a gate onto a signposted cycle track heading northwest. A left turn after 30m, down through the woodland, brings you to the main cycle trail. Here, turn left for Cannop Wharf and follow the trail to the road (B4226). Cross straight over and 50m after the trail joins the road to Cannop car park, opposite a gate, bear right onto a woodland path which runs parallel to the road. This trail makes for pleasant walking and soon reaches the first of the ponds at Cannop and a picnic site. The ponds were formed in 1827 by the damming of the stream that runs through the Cannop Valley. The intention was that they would provide power for the iron furnaces that were then in use at Parkend. The scheme

SPEECH HOUSE LOOP

◀ Cannop Ponds

was not a commercial success and the ponds were given over to birds and other wildlife.

Pass through the car park and at the rear, just beyond the gate on the cycle trail, again bear right to a path on the edge of the pond (or stay on the cycle trail if you prefer). At the far end of the second pond, rejoin the cycle trail at a five-way junction. Here, take the Gloucestershire Way Path (GWP) sharp left through a gate heading northeast up into the woodland of Russell's Inclosure. In 500m, arrive at a crosspaths and turn left. Now head north for 600m and, beyond a dip, turn right (east) to climb between an older plantation on the left and a newer one on the right on a broad track. As the track levels out, reach a junction and turn left (north) across level ground with forestry on the left and cleared ground on the right. After 400m, at a fork, bear left into woodland and soon descend for 500m, muddy in places, to cross a stile and fence. Now turn right (northeast) and follow a path through open woodland, passing the 'Mahony' beech tree, to the Speech House.

This building, now a hotel, and the stone cross on the opposite side of the road mark the traditional centre of the Forest of Dean. The Speech Court is still held here, presided over by the Forest Verderers whose role is to look after the venison (wild animals) and the vert (shelters). Today the power of the Verderers is much reduced since the time of Charles II when the Speech House was built, though the position is still held for life.

From the cross, continue on the GWP for 50m and then, leaving the route, turn left (southwest) through a gate. Now follow the clear path through woodland, staying roughly parallel to the road down to the buildings at Beechenhurst.

Soudley Bridge and the Old Dean Road

Distance 2.5km **Time** 45 mins
Terrain woodland paths and lanes
Map OS Explorer OL14 **Access** buses from Cinderford and Lydney stop at the White Horse Inn at the top of Lower Road in Soudley

This route is ideal for those wanting a walk which is quick but full of history in the charming surroundings of a wooded valley.

The village of Soudley is tucked away between the towns of Cinderford and Lydney. Most visitors come to see the Dean Heritage Centre and the Ponds but there is good walking to the south from Soudley Bridge.

At the bottom of Lower Road in Soudley is the old bridge over Soudley Brook by the recreation area, where parking is available. Take the signed Forest Footpath at the rear of the parking area southwest into woodland with Soudley Brook on the right. The path soon bears left away from the brook and heads uphill along the line of what is thought to be a Roman road. There is some doubt as to the exact line of the route the Romans would have taken from Lydney northwards to Ariconium, near the modern town of Ross. However, it is likely that the old Dean Road, which may have predated the Romans, keeps to much the same line. Whatever the origins of the route, some stone surfacing and kerbing can be seen along the path.

After 500m, you reach a modern forest road. Here, bear left along the verge for 100m before turning left along another forest road towards Bradley Hill. In 300m, you come to the edge of the woodland and a clearing dotted with houses.

Soudley Bridge and the Old Dean Road

◂ Leaf fall in woods on Bradley Hill

Continue ahead uphill for 150m to the top of the rise and into woodland again. The woodland in this area is well worth visiting in springtime for the covering of bluebells.

At the track junction, turn left and head north with views back over Soudley. The track soon descends gently to join the lane on its left before passing through a barrier, where it becomes a fenced path and starts to descend the ridge with a small ravine on the left and old quarry workings to the right. These can be explored by climbing over a stile. A little further on, at a path junction, take the right fork down through the woodland. At the bottom of the slope, bear round to the left, passing above Dean Heritage Centre, and in 250m cross an old packhorse stone footbridge over Soudley Brook. At this point, the Dean Heritage Centre can be reached on a path to the right alongside the brook.

From the bridge, continue ahead to emerge onto Tramway Road. In the early 19th century, horse-drawn tramroads were developed in the Forest of Dean to transport coal and ironstone to local ironworks. This tramroad linked the area, via a tunnel through Bradley Hill, to the River Severn at Bullo, to the east, and Lydney, to the south. Now turn left and follow the lane downhill to another bridge over the brook. Just after the bridge, turn right onto a pleasant grassy path which leads back beside the brook to Soudley Bridge itself.

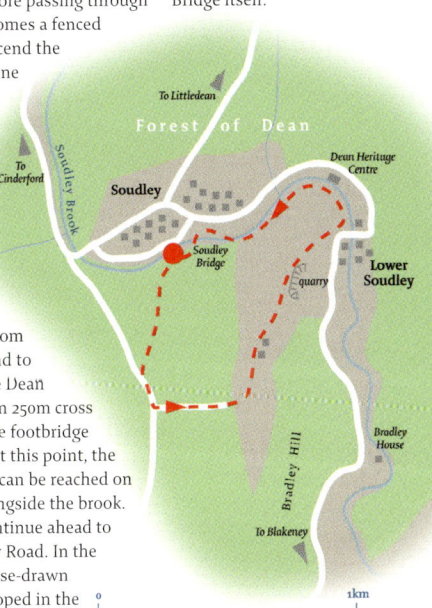

St Briavels and the Slade Brook

Distance 5km **Time** 1 hour 30
Terrain lanes, fields and woodland
Map OS Explorer OL14 **Access** limited buses to St Briavels from Monmouth and Chepstow

Enjoy the sense of history and nature on this short walk from the Dean's most famous village.

St Briavels is today one of the best known villages in the area. It stands high up above the Wye Valley and its commanding position echoes its importance as the one-time administrative and judicial centre of the Forest of Dean. The Norman castle and church dominate the village centre and exude a great sense of history. You can even stay in the castle – it has been a youth hostel for more than 50 years – though in former times a visit was not so sought after. You could be arraigned before the Court of Mine Law, had you usurped the privileges of the Free Miners who claimed the sole right to mine in the Dean, and if found guilty you might even have been thrown in the dungeon. The village itself was famous for its quarrels – though in the form of bolts for crossbows.

From the castle, walk down Mork Road past the church and in 400m, at the hairpin bend, bear right down Mork Lane. This follows the line of the medieval road

St Briavels and the Slade Brook

northwards to Redbrook and gives good views over the valley ahead. Descend, steeply at times, to the ford through the Slade Brook and on to the road beyond – the house to the left under which the brook flows is Sladbrook, a fine early 19th-century former mill, and across the road are the gables and mullioned windows of Mork Farm, which date back to the early 17th century.

Here, turn right along the road and just beyond the bend take the footpath right through a gate into a strip of woodland back towards the Slade Brook. The alder-lined brook takes you eastwards over fields into woodland. Here, in the brook's streambed, begins a spectacular if easily-missed series of tufa dams, one of the longest in Britain. This remarkable rock is formed when limestone dissolved in water is deposited on rocks and debris.

At a footbridge in the woodland, cross to the other bank and a little way up, where the path gives out, recross to the original side, picking a path through the trees to reach a forestry track which crosses the brook where a side stream joins.

Now follow the broad track to the right of the brook as it climbs uphill and leaves the woodland to reach Bearse Farm, which stands in an area inhabited by humans since Neolithic times – one of the finest examples of a polished flint axe was found near here.

Just before the farm, take the footpath on the right which rises between horse paddocks. Beyond, enter woodland and bear left across a dip. Leave the woodland and go uphill towards Bushyard Barn, passing to the right. Now aim for the far right corner of this long field, with the tower of St Briavels Church away on the left. Head across the next two fields, following the fence on the left and, where the fence turns sharp left towards the church tower, bear left across the field to a gate and stile in the wall opposite. Here, cross onto Mork Road once more and turn left back up the hill to St Briavels.

◀ St Briavels Castle

Woolaston Ridge and Severn views

Distance 8km **Time** 2 hours 30
Terrain fields and woodland
Map OS Explorer OL14 **Access** buses from Chepstow stop on the A48 by Church Lane in Woolaston

From near the banks of the Severn, traverse ancient lanes and fields and climb up onto the southern slopes of the Forest of Dean.

The walk starts south of Woolaston village, where there is a car park and toilets on the north side of the A48 (GR589992). Turn left onto the road at the rear of the parking area and left again along the lane to the Church of St Andrew. This impressive building stands at some distance to the southwest of where the modern village has grown up, but it is thought that the site is actually close to the line of the Roman road that runs from Gloucester to Caerleon. At this point, it passed just to the north of the church before joining the modern line of the A48 just above Stroat, whose name may be a corruption of 'Street'.

At the rear of the churchyard, go through a gate and pass to the right of the farm buildings into a small field. At the far end, turn left onto a green lane which leads to a footbridge over Black Brook and into a field – this could well be the line of the Roman road. Where the hedge bends left bear right through a gateway and down to a lane, formerly known as Millin Lane, which leads right uphill to High Woolaston Farm.

At the bend, turn left past farm buildings and then right along a short walled track to fields. With Piccadilly Brook to the left, make for the woodland in the top left corner of the second field. Here reputedly stands the tallest poplar tree in the Forest of Dean. Cross a stile into chestnut woodland and turn left on a small path through Ashwell Grove, which

Woolaston Ridge and Severn views

◂ Stone barn at High Woolaston Farm

soon leads up to a forestry track. Here, bear right uphill for 500m before turning left onto the Gloucestershire Way (GW).

Follow the route out of the woodland, across a lane and along the bottom edge of a field, with good views to the south. To the north is an area called Poor's Allotment, a reminder that this was once open common, used for essential grazing and coppicing. Go through a small copse and onto a lane and, after 400m where the lane bends back left, leave the GW and take a path left down through ancient coppiced woodland. This is known as Ridley Bottom and is now a nature reserve managed by Gloucestershire Wildlife Trust. In 200m, where the woodland ends, cross a stile on the right, and head for the top of the sloping field to the pool of Slade Well. Cross the stile 50m beyond and bear right in a southerly direction to the bottom corner of the field and onto Rosemary Lane.

Go left for 150m and just after the left bend take the path left down fields to Stroat, dog-legging left, then right after the first field to pick up a stream down to the A48 main road. It is thought that this path follows the line of a prehistoric trackway, which continues all the way down to the Severn, where a stone slab called the Broad Stone marks an ancient crossing point.

At the road, turn left and then left again through the buildings of Stroat Farm, bearing right up to a field gate. The final section of the walk follows the line of an old lane that was still in use in the 18th century, but has now been largely lost beneath the plough. Go diagonally right up this field and along the top of the next one onto the lane past Ashwell Grange. Now head down and up fields, across two streams (the second one is Piccadilly Brook), in a NNE direction to reach High Woolaston Farm once more. From here the outward route will take you back to the start.

Rising steeply from Monmouth to the village of Trellech, this upland area stretches all the way to Chepstow. From its plateau, there are striking views westwards across the Usk Valley towards the Black Mountains. On the eastern side steep slopes and gushing streams plunge down into the Wye Gorge and were once sites for the industries of iron smelting, wire-working and paper production. Farmland and woodland, both ancient and modern, are criss-crossed by lanes and trackways, connecting a large number of hamlets and settlements, many of which date back to a Norman foundation. Indeed, the medieval village of Trellech was one of the most important towns in Wales. The plateau still retains a sense of seclusion and you can wander for miles in varied and tranquil surroundings.

The Trellech to Chepstow Plateau

1. **The secluded slopes of Cwmcarfan** — 82
   Nestling in the western scarp of the Trellech plateau, this secluded cwm is perfect walking country

2. **Beacon Hill from Trellech** — 84
   A classic round from an historic Welsh village where there is plenty to explore

3. **Trellech and Hygga** — 86
   An up and down route full of interest to the south of an historic village

4. **Wolvesnewton and Gaer Fawr** — 88
   Visit the largest hillfort in Gwent on this feisty round of the ridges above a charming hamlet

5. **Devauden and Chepstow Park Wood** — 90
   Forest tracks and green lanes rise and fall on this route above the Fedw Valley

6. **St Arvans and Itton Court** — 92
   Follow a medieval route across fields before circling an historic manor house and grounds

7. **The stones of Gray Hill** — 94
   The climb may be steep and short but the views go on and on – save this one for a clear day

THE TRELLECH TO CHEPSTOW PLATEAU

The secluded slopes of Cwmcarfan

Distance 7km **Time** 2 hours 30
Terrain field paths, lanes and woodland tracks; a steep climb up to the ridge
Map OS Explorer OL14 **Access** buses from Monmouth and Chepstow stop on the B4293 at Five Trees bus stop, mid-route

Nestling below the ridge that runs along to Trellech, this walk is full of delight, and a great place for an evening stroll to watch the sun set.

Tucked away in the folds of the hills which face west into Wales, there is a far greater sense of remoteness at Cwmcarfan than the distance of 6km from Monmouth would suggest. Now there are a few houses, some farms and the church of St Cadog. This impressive building stands on an intervening ridge, framed above by the woods of the Trellech plateau, from where a lane circuitously wends its way. The easier approach is from the old A40 road, just to the south of Mitchel Troy, and as you climb away from the valley there is a real sense of entering a forgotten cirque of fields and ridges, though at the end of the 19th century more than 200 people are recorded as living in the parish.

From the church, where there is parking for a few cars, walk back down the hill and in 150m turn right on the track down towards Church Farm. Across Cwmcarfan Brook bear diagonally right up over two fields and then round to the south, before climbing up to the east of Cwmcarfan Court to meet its driveway. Here, a right turn onto the lane leads uphill for 1km to the road junction with good views back westwards. Just to the right can be seen the settlement of Craig-y-dorth, reputedly the site of Owain Glyndwr's defeat of Henry IV's English forces in 1404 – they were chased all the way down the far side of the hill to the Monnow Gate at Monmouth.

Now bear right, passing the entrance to

◀ Field trees near Craig-y-dorth

Caer Llan, along the quiet lane up to the B4293. Cross this to follow the minor road towards Chapel Farm and at the bend, a little before the farm, take the field-path on the right down to the road again. Here, turn left along the grassy verge for 350m (the bus stops along here at Five Trees), taking the second footpath on the right along a private road into woodland. Pass the entrance to High Glanau and Glanau Lodge and 500m from the road, where the track bends right, continue ahead. Descend just beyond the gables of Glanau Cottages to a barrier, where there is an old boundary stone.

Here, fork right down across a stream and turn right onto a bridleway that leads through mixed woodland. The path climbs a little and curves round to the left before descending southwest to join a forestry track. Bear right downhill on the track and, where the Forestry Commission land ends, keep ahead for 200m and then turn right down a field with a cottage on the left to reach the track beyond. Here, turn right onto the track and descend past stables. Now follow the pleasant country lane for another 1km back down to Cwmcarfan and enjoy the views westwards as the hills of the Black Mountains appear through the gaps in the hedges.

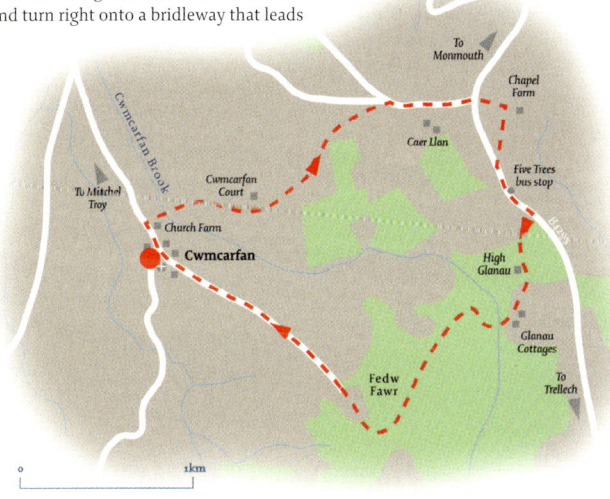

Beacon Hill from Trellech

Distance 4km **Time** 1 hour 30
Terrain fields, lanes and tracks
Map OS Explorer OL14 **Access** buses to
Trellech from Monmouth and Chepstow

Be enchanted by this ancient village and the views from the nearby high ground of Beacon Hill.

Today Trellech is a vibrant village which has a church with a famous octagonal tower, a welcoming pub, the Lion Inn, and a primary school. In the 13th and 14th centuries it was one of the largest towns in Wales. However, the exact whereabouts of the medieval village is the subject of competing local theories. One locates it beneath current buildings surrounding the church and the former motte and bailey castle; another points to recent archaeological finds and surveys in fields a little to the south of the modern village centre, in the area around the Virtuous Well.

Opposite the church, a lane between the Babington Centre and the pub leads away from the village. At the left-hand bend take the signed footpath on the right across a field. Bear diagonally left and pass through a gap in the fence to join a tractor track on the field edge heading towards Upper Barn. In the field before the barn, cross into the field on the left and follow the waymarks up past the barn, bearing slightly left. Just beyond a brick stables, take the right fork up over fields to Beacon Road.

Here, a dog-leg right for 30m, then left onto a bridleway leads through woodland. After 100m, at a crosspaths, turn right onto a forest track and pass through a vehicle barrier. The track climbs a little and brings you out onto the cleared area near the broad top of Beacon Hill. The geology of this area is markedly different from much of the lower Wye Valley – the peaty soil is dotted with white stones which hint at the quartz conglomerate rock underlying this

◀ The Virtuous Well at Trellech

heathy acidic podzol. It provides ideal growing conditions for a rare and local bramble, *Rubus Trelleckensis*, which is known on only a few sites in this part of the Wye Valley.

Continue a little beyond a cattle grid and take the first track right uphill. Pass through a gate and into woodland and soon arrive at Beacon Hill viewpoint, where there is a useful information board and a picnic table. The very top of the hill, marked by a triangulation point, is in the trees away to the left of the onward path. Now follow the path downhill through woodland to a car park. Here, turn left along Beacon Road and then right at the junction. After 500m, look out for the sign on the right for the Virtuous Well.

Known also as St Anne's Well, it is a natural spring which was reputed from medieval times to have the power to heal a variety of ailments, such as scurvy and abdominal pains. If you are here on midsummer's eve, keep an eye out for the fairies, which are said to dance near the spring and drink its water from harebell cups. From here, cross the bridge and head left over fields on a waymarked path to the back of the village car park.

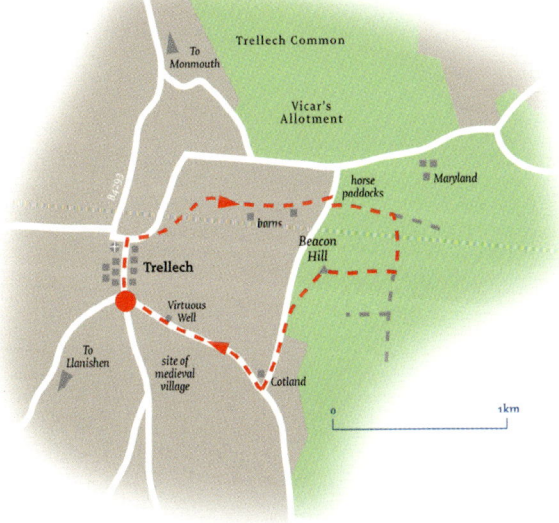

Trellech and Hygga

Distance 7km **Time** 2 hours
Terrain field, woodland paths and lanes
Map OS Explorer OL14 **Access** buses to Trellech from Monmouth and Chepstow

From the medieval village of Trellech, on the high ground between the Wye and Usk Valleys, this undulating route passes a number of places of interest, including some standing stones, a 17th-century furnace and an Iron Age hillfort.

From the car park, follow signs to Harold's Stones on the southern edge of the village. One local legend has it that in a contest with the devil these stones were hurled by Jack O'Kent, a huge giant, from Ysgyryd Fawr (Skirrid Mountain), a hill over 16km to the northwest. Archaeologists date their positioning from the Bronze Age. At any rate, they gave the village its name (*tre* – 'three', *llech* – 'stone').

From the stones, go along the road for 50m, away from the village, and at the bend take the tree-lined path on the right signed Penarth Brook & Llanishen. It immediately crosses Penarth Brook and in 200m veers left and soon enters an open field. Bear to the left downhill and in 200m, where a sidestream from the left meets the brook, cross the stream and head up the slope a little way before bearing right uphill along a fence on the right. At the top of the field between two stiles take the permissive path into Woolpitch Wood, signed Trellech Furnace.

Go downhill through the conifer woodland and cross Penarth Brook once more on a footbridge. Turn left to follow the brook's right bank downhill, in 250m passing the former site of Trellech Furnace in a clearing – here from the 17th century iron ore was smelted to make pig iron, the nearby stream being used to power a

waterwheel which operated the bellows of the furnace. After another 250m, where a sidestream comes down from the right, cross the brook and follow the track uphill as the brook drops away on the right. As fields open out on the left, cross a stile into woodland and descend on a meandering path to a lane by a house.

Turn left and follow the sunken lane uphill, steeply at first, past Pant-glas House to the B4293 road. Cross over and take the lane and bridleway, signed Hygga and Parkhouse. The lane descends to Hygga with views left to Beacon Hill, ahead to St Briavels Common and right to the woods above Tintern. The buildings at Hygga date back to the 16th century (there are old barns and a restored dovecote visible) and the land was once worked by the monks of Tintern Abbey, Hygga being the site of a former manor house. This area is also the source of the Anghidi River which eventually plunges down to Tintern – its tree-lined course is visible to the southeast. Just beyond the farm is a huge hollow sycamore tree by a remarkable walled walk-in drinking trough for horses.

The bridleway now descends and rises with a clear view left to a rounded hill, the site of an Iron Age hillfort, before descending again to a stream. Turn left and follow the stream for 100m, then go straight ahead, with the stream on the right, on a path signed Trelleck Cross, ignoring the bridleway as it turns right uphill. At the top of the field, cross a stile above the fenced-off Ffynnon Gaer ('Spring of the Fort') and follow the path across the field as it bears right uphill and becomes a sunken way which leads up to Trelleck Cross. At the lane, turn right and pass the base of an old cross just before the crossroads. Turn left along the lane for just over 500m and bear left again at a junction to reach Trellech.

◀ Mown hay near Pant-glas House

Wolvesnewton and Gaer Fawr

Distance 7km **Time** 2 hours 30
Terrain fields and lanes; some steep slopes
Map OS Explorer OL14
Access no public transport to the start

Enter the lair overlooked by one of the largest, but least known, hillforts in Gwent.

Wolvesnewton is hidden among the steep slopes and narrow lanes between the high ground of the Trellech plateau and the Usk Valley. The curious English name stems from a local family called Wolf, prominent in the 14th century, rather than from the recollection of any mythical pack of wild beasts. The origin of the church dates from earlier still and its dedication to St Thomas a Becket firmly links the area to the Normans. There are no graves on the northern side of the church and the medieval cross has been converted into a war memorial. Now sparsely populated, this cirque of ridges must once have been thronging with busy rural life. Indeed, the area's occupation stretches back to the Iron Age and even Neolithic times.

Take the lane westwards just in front of the church and soon pass between some houses to fields beyond. Cross through six fields in a westerly direction for 1km, over the brow of the hill and down to Nantygelli Farm. Gold is apparently still to be found in the stream near here. A former servant at the farm was reputedly frightened out of his wits by a ghostly apparition which ordered the poor man to dispose of a purse containing 12 guineas in a nearby stream. This was to prevent the ghost's wife from getting hold

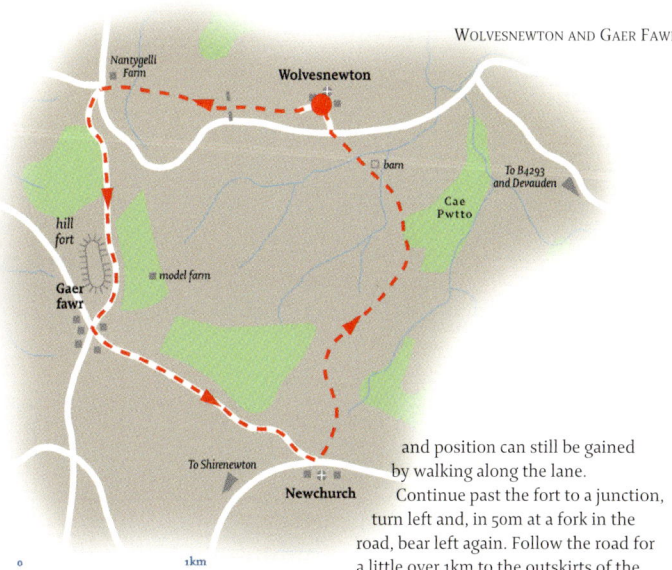

of the small fortune. When the story got out people searched high and low, but in vain; the gold was never found.

Pass to the left of the farm and climb the field beyond to the road. Go over the crossroads up the single-track road, which leads steeply uphill for 750m where the earthworks to Gaer Fawr hillfort can be seen on the right beyond Camp House. This hillfort is one of the most extensive in this part of Wales and occupies a commanding position with steep slopes on all but the south side. It is thought there was a double rampart which met in the southeast corner and encircled the west side, with possibly a third outer ring lower down. The fort itself lies on private land, but an idea of its impressive size and position can still be gained by walking along the lane.

Continue past the fort to a junction, turn left and, in 50m at a fork in the road, bear left again. Follow the road for a little over 1km to the outskirts of the ridge-top hamlet of Newchurch – it has a small church dedicated to St Peter, set on the ridge with good views of the surrounding countryside.

Take the path northwards 100m before the road junction in Newchurch, and weave your way down over six fields to Cae Pwtto Wood (in the first field follow the right-hand hedge, in the second the left, bear left along the top of the third, in the fourth bear right down to the corner of a copse, and through the next two head northeast to a stile into the wood). The path meanders through the west side of the wood for 200m and then into a field to descend to a barn and a track: this leads up to Lower House Farm. Here, cross the road and climb the lane to return to Wolvesnewton Church.

◀ Above Wolvesnewton looking west to the Black Mountains

Devauden and Chepstow Park Wood

Distance 6km **Time** 2 hours
Terrain woodland paths and lanes over undulating ground **Map** OS Explorer OL14
Access buses to Devauden from Monmouth and Chepstow

Venture into the one-time haunts of highwaymen before discovering the hidden Fedw Valley.

Chepstow Park Wood was once part of a great swathe of woodland stretching in an arc from Chepstow to Trellech and Monmouth and up the Monnow Valley on the Welsh side, and round to Ross, through the current Forest of Dean, and all the way to the Severn below Gloucester. Over the centuries, the woods have been enclosed for coppicing and pasturing, and many, such as Chepstow Park Wood, are now managed by the Forestry Commission, who are gradually restoring the plantations of the 20th century to mixed woodland.

The walk starts at the village green in Devauden, where John Wesley preached his first sermon in Wales in October 1739 to a congregation of hundreds. A path on the south side of the green, to the right of the village hall, leads into Chepstow Park Wood (signposted for Itton). After 250m, take the second path on the left between conifer plantations and then in another 300m, at a forestry track, dog-leg left, then right into mixed woodland to continue in

DEVAUDEN AND CHEPSTOW PARK WOOD

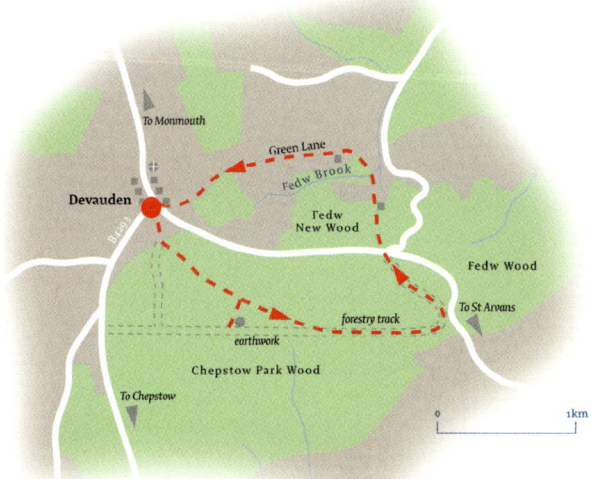

a southeasterly direction beside a tumbledown drystone wall on the right. Soon pass over a crosspaths (it is possible to detour right here for a few hundred metres to the site of some small earthworks) and in just over 500m, at a broad forestry track, turn left and almost immediately, at the fork, again bear left downhill, with deciduous woodland on the left, conifers away on the right and views ahead to Gaer Hill. In 500m, at a fork in the track, bear left to continue downhill to the road.

Cross over into the deciduous woodland of New Wood and descend northwards down a sunken lane to a crosstrack. Dog-leg left for 30m, then right to continue downhill to the houses and lanes of the hidden Fedw Valley. Here, you'll find a scattering of houses enclosed by the steep slopes of the valley, much of which is covered in conifer plantation, but the name Y Fedw means The Birches and hints at the older woods that used to cover the area. Many of the walled lanes were probably made by squatters who illegally settled here as woodsmen and workers at the nearby Tintern wireworks.

At the junction turn right and in 50m, at the bend, turn left up a sunken lane which soon curves round to the left and passes a house where it becomes a path between fields. Continue uphill for a little over 500m, with views across the Fedw Valley, until the path emerges onto a lane which leads back into Devauden.

◂ Logging in Chepstow Park Wood

St Arvans and Itton Court

Distance 7.5km **Time** 2 hours
Terrain field paths and lanes
Map OS Explorer OL14 **Access** buses to
St Arvans from Monmouth and Chepstow

Follow the medieval route to one of Tintern Abbey's granges before circling the countryside surrounding Itton Court.

St Arvans is easily bypassed on the road north of Chepstow through the Wye Valley. However, it pays to spend a little time exploring the village. The walk starts from the restored Victorian fountain at the A466 junction. Walk through the village and turn left up Church Lane to the Church of St Arvan which is worth seeing, not least for its unusual octagonal tower and its curious dormer windows.

Beyond the church, follow the lane round the bend, then bear left onto a fenced path that leads between the recreation area and fields. Cross into the field ahead through a lever-board stile and down along the fence into a slight dip. In the next field bear right and follow a line of oak trees, which mark the line of the old medieval way to Rogerstone Grange, one of the most important former granges of Tintern Abbey.

The field on the right, to the east of the grange, used to be known as St John's Mead and a number of limekilns were purposely sited here, on what is a geological faultline. The underlying rock to the south of here is limestone, with shale to the north which changes to old red sandstone near the ridge.

At the grange, turn left along the track for 50m, then right along a fenced path to pass to the south of the buildings and into the field beyond. Now follow the right-hand field-hedge and in the second field bear right through a gap and along the eastern edge of Pilmoore Wood for 50m, before crossing a stile left into the wood: this is good for snowdrops and

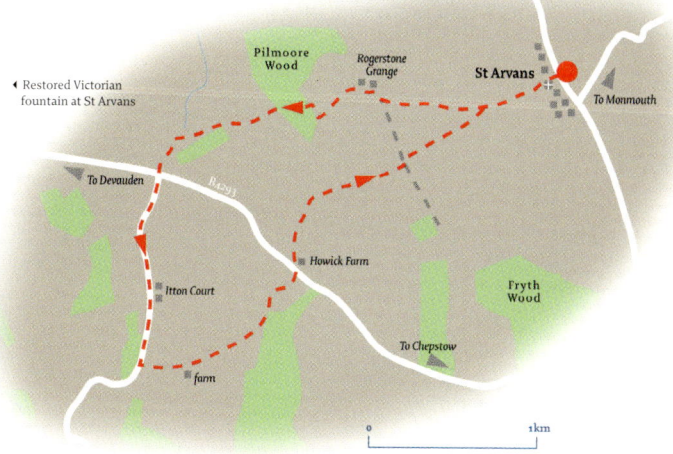

bluebells in spring, though it can be muddy underfoot, a sign that the underlying free-draining limestone has been left behind. The path now heads westwards up through the wood before crossing three more fields (in the second field bear right over a stile into the adjacent field) to descend to a track which bears left past houses down to a crossroads with the B4293.

Here, take the rising lane opposite, passing Itton Court after 500m, to Itton Church. Dedicated to St Deiniol, it sits close by the former manor house of Itton Court and was much restored in the 19th century. Look for the large squared blocks in the tower which are made from the local grey limestone and in the porch the coat of arms with the Latin motto *Gratus Si Amicus* – 'Welcome, if a friend'. Continue beyond the church for 400m before turning left along another pleasant lane with good views back to Itton Court and in just over 1km reach the B4293 again at Howick Farm.

Set above the level of the road, the stone farmhouse gives the impression of great age – its origins date from the 16th century. Pass to the left of the farm buildings into the fields beyond and cross the first two in a northerly direction, heading for the mast on Gaer Hill. Then bear right (ENE) over the brow of the hill along three field edges, with views ahead to St Arvans, to the track which leads north to Rogerstone Grange.

Here, dog-leg across this track and along the edge of the next field down into the dip. Bear left up the next field and reach the lever-board stile once again. From here, retrace the outward route back to St Arvans.

The stones of Gray Hill

Distance 3km **Time** 1 hour **Terrain** open slopes and forest tracks; the ascent of Gray Hill is steep **Map** OS Explorer OL14 **Access** no public transport to the start

Climb one of the best natural viewpoints in South Wales and wander amongst ancient stones and woodland.

This route provides an ideal short walk to be combined with local sightseeing, or a leisurely stroll in good weather to make the best of the views. The walk starts at Foresters' Oaks car park and picnic site on the Usk road north of the village of Llanvair Discoed; it's above Wentwood Reservoir on the edge of Wentwood Forest. There are a number of picnic benches overlooking the reservoir.

It is salutary to think that until the early 19th century the Foresters' Oaks were in no way connected with recreation. It was here that the medieval Forest Courts were held and the great oaks themselves served a capital purpose for those unlucky enough to be caught poaching or stealing from the forest.

From the car park, bear right across the road up a surfaced track for 400m, past some houses where the path narrows. Beyond the houses leave the path, which contours the hill, and turn left through a gate onto Gray Hill Common, climbing steeply with views down to the reservoir and beyond to the Severn Estuary.

At the top, the panoramic views on a clear day are stunning and it is quite

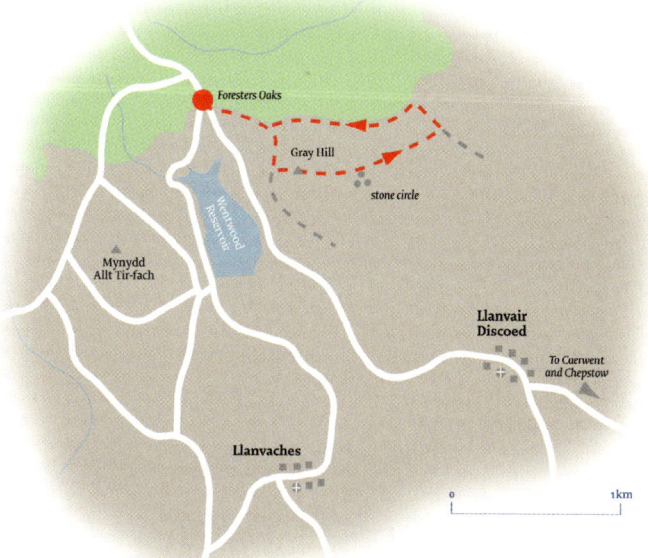

possible to see right across the Severn Estuary and beyond. Bear left and walk northeast along the ridge for just under 1km – it is worth detouring off this path to hunt for the Bronze Age stones that cover the top of the hill. There are three burial cairns, two standing stones and a stone circle, though trees and scrub now cover the once open hillside. There are also good views north and west over Wentwood Forest, the largest planted ancient woodland site in Wales. After a century of being planted with fast-growing coniferous trees, the forest was purchased by the Woodland Trust in 2006 with the aim of returning it to its former broadleaf splendour.

To continue the walk, descend gradually to a path junction and turn left, heading more steeply downhill for 200m. The view soon opens out to the right across a field and, where the woodland starts again on the right, turn left onto a gently rising path which skirts the northern slopes of Gray Hill Common.

In 300m, at the top of the rise, the path starts to descend along the edge of forestry woodland, following a line of beech trees with open fields to the left. In another 300m, dog-leg right downhill for 50m into the forestry plantation, then left, and follow the path to a track junction on the outward route. Here, turn right and retrace your steps downhill to Foresters' Oaks.

◀ Rolling farmland north of Gray Hill

Index

Backbury Hill	8
Ballingham	16
Beacon Hill	84
Beechenhurst Lodge	72
Bradley Hill	74
Brockweir	54
Buckstone	68
Cannop	72
Capler Camp	14
Catbrook	52
Chase Wood	20
Chepstow Castle	60, 62
Chepstow Park Wood	90
Cleddon Falls	52
Coldwell Rocks	42
Coppet Hill	42
Coughton	20
Cwmcarfan	82
Devauden	90
Devil's Pulpit, The	56
Dingestow	36
Eagles' Nest, The	58
English Bicknor	44
Foresters' Oaks	94
Fownhope	14
Foy	18
Garway Hill	28
Goodrich	42
Gray Hill	94
Harold's Stones	86
Holme Lacy	12
Hudnalls, The	54
Hygga	86
Itton	92
Jack O'Kent	28
Kentchurch	28
Kilpeck	24
King Arthur's Cave	46
King's Caple	18
Kymin, The	68
Lancaut	62
Littledean	70
Lydbrook	66
Marcle Hill	10
Mitchel Troy	82
Monmouth	34, 38
Mordiford	8
Narth, The	50
Newchurch	89
Newland	48
Offa's Dyke Path	32, 34, 44, 56, 62, 68
Orcop Hill	26
Penallt	38
Piercefield Park	60
Redbrook	48
Ridley Bottom	78
Ross-on-Wye	20
Sellack	18
Seven Sisters	46
Skenfrith	30
Sollers Hope	10
Soudley Bridge	74
Speech House	72
Symonds Yat	46
St Arvans	92
St Briavels	76
Tintern Abbey	58
Trellech	84, 86
Treowen	36
Welsh Bicknor	42
Welshbury Fort	70
Wentwood	94
Wilton	20
Wolvesnewton	88
Woolaston	78
Woolhope	10